GOD AND GUNS IN AMERICA

God and Guns in America

Michael W. Austin

WILLIAM B. EERDMANS PUBLISHING COMPANY
GRAND RAPIDS, MICHIGAN

Wm. B. Eerdmans Publishing Co.
4035 Park East Court SE, Grand Rapids, Michigan 49546
www.eerdmans.com

26 25 24 23 22 21 20   1 2 3 4 5 6 7

ISBN 978-0-8028-7643-0

Library of Congress Cataloging-in-Publication Data

A catalog record for this book is available from
the Library of Congress.

*This book is dedicated to Anita Franklin and Heidi Cortez.
Not only did they survive, they also fight for a world
of righteousness, justice, and peace.*

CONTENTS

Contents

FOREWORD

America stands at a crossroads in its relationships with guns. The status quo seems untenable. On one side, many gun owners want few (or no!) restrictions; on the other side, some want to abolish legal ownership of guns completely.

America's division over guns is most evident in political and religious debate. Political parties are sharply divided. Religious Americans, armed with sacred texts and theological ideas, occupy opposite fields of the dueling ground. Christian evangelicals, especially, are at a precarious crossroads, if not in dangerous crisis.

After traveling the country discussing this subject at length with pastors, church and ministry leaders, academics, and denominational executives, I thought I understood the complexity of the debate. Then something happened. My own twin brother, who is also ordained, drew my attention to a popular Bible product marketed by an unlikely manufacturer, Arizona-based Garrison Grip. Looking at it online, I couldn't believe my eyes. The typical black faux-leather, zippered case had an embossed gold moniker emblazed on the front reading "Holy Bible." Inside, though, you would not find space for the pages of sacred Scripture. Instead, glued to the right inside panel was a pistol holster configured to fit any semiautomatic handgun, and glued to the left inside panel was an elastic holder for a magazine of bullets. The idea was to conceal-carry your weapon and ammo undetected in church or anywhere else. To see if it was indeed genuine, I ordered one. It was.

The Garrison Grip "gun Bible" inadvertently locates this problem squarely where it belongs—at the theological center of evangelicalism. The decision to take into one's hand the power to end human life, the justification for doing so, calculating how to do it effectively, and engaging with public policy that allows for it easily—these considerations raise many questions about God, humankind, how we are to live—or die, for that matter—how we are to treat one another, and how we are to be known and perceived by others. In other words, just about anything concerning guns relates directly or indirectly to something the Bible teaches about how God wishes for us to live—and die.

In this book, Professor Michael Austin carefully examines this theological problem. He treats the question of Christians and guns in relation to the will of God for humanity, what it means to be a faithful disciple of Christ, and the ethical obligations of a Christian.

Reason isn't often cited as an attribute of evangelicals. Yet, reason, as much as emotion, is an attribute of God, and the Creator of our intellectual faculties calls it forth from us in his invitation delivered through the prophet, "Come now, let us reason together, says the LORD" (Isa. 1:18). If the national discussion on guns needs anything, it needs the reasonable approach taken here to counter the highly charged atmosphere generated wherever this topic comes up.

Professor Austin uses God-given reason as his tool to help us find our way through the murky, confusing, sometimes jumbled thread of Bible quotes—too commonly cherry-picked and exploited by both sides of this controversy—while he debunks the circuitous arguments that often follow. A consummate moral philosopher and ethicist, as well as a sincere Christian believer in the evangelical mold, the author helps us immensely with his exhaustive treatment of the complicated and troublesome area of American gun policy and practice. He examines the historical, emotional, theological, and social dimensions of gun ownership, deadly force, self-defense, and the claim by some of a Christian duty to use guns to protect ourselves and others. In every instance, the author presents various and opposing viewpoints, but he never shies away from giving us his own sound analyses and succinct conclusions.

While Austin has produced an excellent and scholarly study, *God and Guns in America* should not be mistaken for an empty academic tome—far from it. His is not simply a theoretical perspective, nor is it based in the hypothetical. He offers facts, statistical data, and verifiable evidence to help us understand the very real-world, concrete, and consequential dimensions to the problem of guns and suggests practical steps to reduce gun violence that can be implemented by individuals, churches, and whole communities. His work is not to lay bare an insurmountable or irresolvable problem, but, instead, to help define the problem with a view toward finding immediate and long-term solutions to it.

This biblical and sociological investigation into guns, violence, and the passions and politics that surround them is both timely and timeless. It is sure to outlast even the most concrete and universal resolutions to this bedeviling problem because at the study's core are much larger, recurring, and permanent questions about the proper exegesis of Scripture, what it means to follow Jesus, the nature and character of God, the meaning of the commandments—especially of the two great commandments of Christ, to love God and love our neighbors as ourselves—and the transcendent virtues of the Sermon on the Mount, including how to love our enemies. This, too, is consistent with Scripture, for "what good is it, my brothers, if someone claims to have faith, but has no deeds?" (James 2:14a).

With insight, brilliance, and conviction, Austin shows us how to match what the Bible, the evidence, and Christian discernment say about God and guns in America with corresponding actions we can undertake to reduce the dangers and suffering that so often attend them.

REV. ROB SCHENCK
President
The Dietrich Bonhoeffer Institute
Washington, DC

PREFACE

I am a Christian, a gun owner, and a professor. I do not live on the West Coast or the East Coast. I live and work in the Bible Belt. Like millions of Americans, I have been around guns all my life. In fact, I owned a gun before I was born. It was a .22 caliber rifle, a youth model. My dad purchased the gun for four dollars while my mom was pregnant. I have good memories of firing that single-shot rifle as a kid. I also remember my dad's gun cabinet in our family room, and later his gun safe, filled with shotguns for trap shooting, skeet shooting, and sporting clays. There were lots and lots of guns in my childhood home, handguns included. I grew up as a gun guy in a gun family.

One of my clearest and most vivid childhood memories is of a pheasant-hunting trip in western Kansas. We went out with several others, walking the field in a line. There was an ice storm that day, and we had to battle the layers of ice that kept forming on our shotguns. I am not sure how many pheasants I shot that day. I do remember at least one successful shot and the pride I felt at hitting the target at distance.

Now, as an adult, I only occasionally go shooting. In fact, it has been a couple of years now, mainly because I have other interests. I am not afraid of guns. I am not antigun, whatever that means. I am also not a pacifist. *I am concerned about violence.* I am even more concerned with the cavalier attitude many Americans—Christians and non-Christians alike—have toward violence and weapons.

As I write, the American gun debate rages on. Gun violence continues apace. Volleys and salvos pierce the air, leaving real victims, both physical and emotional. Families feud. Friendships break down. Anger flares. Reason becomes a stranger. Legal and moral issues become a jumbled mess. We have a problem. It is time to return to the table and talk. Such honesty requires frank self-examination, earnest listening, and real conversation.

During the time I've been writing this book and sending chapters to my editor, two notable books have appeared: *Beating Guns: Hope for People Who Are Weary of Violence*, by Shane Claiborne and Michael Martin, and *Common Ground: Talking about Gun Violence in America*, by Donald V. Gaffney. I have learned from and recommend both.

My goals in this book are twofold. First, I am going to argue that Christians in the United States of America need to carefully rethink the use of weapons, guns included. Measured, thoughtful, and robust discussion is long overdue. I hope to contribute to the discussion through biblical, theological, philosophical, and ethical arguments. Second, I am going to argue that the United States needs to implement more effective laws and strategies for limiting gun violence. There is almost universal agreement that *some forms* of weapons control should be in place (e.g., certain people and types of weapons should be restricted). The question is, what types of regulations, rules, and restrictions? My first goal—the development of Christian character—is a moral goal; the second aim of the book—legislative reform—is a legal goal. We can improve.

In general, I hope this book elevates our conversation and debate about violence and weapons in the United States. I hope to help improve our collective thoughts about guns, violence, and gun ownership. Throughout, I attempt to be fair. You may or may not agree with me. But I want you to sense my own integrity. I intend to be an honest broker of information and arguments. In the pages that follow, I provide important background information. These relevant data provide deeper understanding. My hope is that regardless of your personal beliefs about guns, you will be better informed and more aware of the issues and arguments relevant to your beliefs after you read this book than you were before you read it.

But to be clear, providing information is not my only goal here. In my opinion, the status quo with respect to guns in America is unsustainable and unacceptable. Violence cannot remain our ready solution to problems. Many people are all too willing to turn to violence as an immediate solution. There are many other possibilities for resolving conflict. Other people seem to regard the Second Amendment almost as Holy Writ. For Christians who happen to be Americans, the Constitution and the Bill of Rights—including the Second Amendment—are of course very important documents. But they are not what is most fundamentally important in this debate. For Christians, the pledge of ultimate allegiance is to Jesus, not to any government or nation. Jesus's life and teachings are of signal significance. We must start there. If there is a conflict between Christian teaching and the Second Amendment, then so much the worse for the Second Amendment.

Broadly, this book is intended for anyone interested in considering these issues in more depth and understanding them from within a Christian point of view. This book is for people who have never owned a gun. This book is also for the people at the gun range and those sitting in hunting blinds at dawn. If you own a gun and love God, this book is for you. If you hate guns and love God, this book is for you. This book is not primarily aimed at professors, though I think much of it will be useful to them. Further exploration of the resources contained in the notes will be especially helpful for those who are interested in exploring any issue in more depth and detail.

However, I am not naïve about the *actual* audience of the book. Many pacifists will not be pleased with many conclusions. Likewise, members of the National Rifle Association (NRA) will be dissatisfied. Yet, I hope both groups will read with profit. However, there are millions and millions of Americans between the two poles. I write for them.

In chapter 1, we briefly explore the history of guns and the Second Amendment in America. It turns out that the truth is different from, and a little more complicated than, the standard story. We also examine the diverse views that Christians in America hold about guns and gun culture.

In chapter 2, we make the case that there is a moral right to own a gun. We also make the case that there are clearly limits to that right. If you cannot exercise the right in a responsible manner, then you forfeit that right.

Chapter 3 reveals the most prominent lies and bad arguments

in our ricocheting gun debate. Our discourse is often frustrating and apparently fruitless.

In chapter 4, the focus shifts to questions related to violence, guns, and the Christian faith. Here we consider some very pointed questions about the relationship between faith and gun violence.

In chapter 5, we examine appeals to the Bible in the gun debate. The Bible is often misinterpreted and misused in such contexts.

In chapter 6, we consider the impact of guns and gun violence on character. This tragic result is often ignored in the gun debates. For Christians, Jesus is our moral exemplar and our ideal. We seek to embody the virtues of Christ.

Finally, chapter 7 answers the question, "What can we *do* about gun violence in America?" The answer goes well beyond thoughts and prayers.

ACKNOWLEDGMENTS

Many people contributed to the book you hold in your hands. I'm grateful to Melanie Cogdill, who first gave me an opportunity to write about these issues for a wider audience. Rob Schenck's life and work continue to be an inspiration to me, and his encouragement throughout the process was invaluable. Thanks as well to everyone at Eerdmans, especially Trevor Thompson. This book is much better, thanks to his keen editorial eye, hard work, and vision for the project. Finally, thanks go to my wife, Dawn, and our daughters Haley, Emma, and Sophie. Being a part of our family continues to be the greatest joy of my life.

1

GOD, GUNS, AND AMERICA

Lori Gilbert Kaye. Riley Howell. Kendrick Castillo. Three heroes who gave their lives to protect others from gun violence. Kaye, a sixty-year-old wife and mother, shielded her rabbi from a gunman at her synagogue near San Diego. She was fatally shot, saving her rabbi's life. Howell, a twenty-one-year-old college student, charged a gunman in a classroom at the University of North Carolina at Charlotte, saving the lives of many. Castillo, an eighteen-year-old high school student at STEM School Highlands Ranch, lunged at the school shooter. His actions saved the lives of many students, but he was fatally shot.[1]

Over an eleven-day period in the spring of 2019, these three martyrs heroically gave their lives to prevent gun violence. We marvel at their courage. We wonder if we would do the same. We lament that these shootings keep happening. We must also ask ourselves some important questions. How many more martyrs must be sacrificed? How many more of these heroes will we need? Unless drastic changes occur, recent history gives us little reason to hope that the need for such heroes will subside. More lives will be lost, more families devastated, more people traumatized.

On May 18, 2018, eight students and two teachers were killed at Santa Fe High School outside of Houston. Another thirteen were injured. The shooter used both a shotgun and a handgun to commit these terrible crimes. The Santa Fe shooting was the seventeenth school shooting of 2018 in the United States in which someone was injured or killed. When asked by a reporter if there was a part of her that thought this wasn't real, that this wouldn't happen at her school, seventeen-year-old Paige Curry said, "No, there wasn't. It's been happening everywhere. I've always kind of felt like eventually it was going to happen here, too."[2] Unfortunately, she was right. And, tragically, others share Paige's fear, and even more tragically, will share her experience. Gun violence continues to sound its steady rounds.

On October 27, 2018, an individual entered the Tree of Life Synagogue in Pittsburgh, murdering eleven people and wounding six. Rabbi Jeffrey Meyers, interviewed on CNN, was asked if he feared that something like this could occur at his synagogue. He said, "I never thought this could happen in my synagogue. Ever."[3] But it did. Unfortunately, he was wrong. And, tragically, others will mistakenly believe it will never happen in a place they love.

We know mass shootings are a problem. Columbine. Sandy Hook. Parkland. Charleston. Sutherland Springs. Las Vegas. Orlando. Virginia Tech. Aurora. San Bernardino. And between the time I write these words at my desk and when you read them in the pages of this book, undoubtedly more will be added to this ever-growing and tragic list.

Mass shootings receive a lot of attention in the media. However, the vast majority of deaths via firearms occur on a smaller scale. Husbands shoot their wives. Parents shoot their children. Children accidentally discharge guns. Thousands of people take their own lives with a gun every year. Data from the Centers for Disease Control—which considers all deaths by gun violence—reveals that 39,773 people died in 2017 from gun violence, an increase of over 1,100 from 2016 and of over 10,000 since 1999.[4] (By comparison, in 2016 there were 37,133 deaths due to motor vehicle accidents.)[5] Only 346 of the deaths by gun violence were due to mass-shooting incidents.[6] On average, another 89,000 people suffer gun injuries each year.[7] Over 8,000 children annually visit an emergency room due to injuries involving guns.[8]

The Great American Gun Debate

It has been rightly observed that in the United States, "the public debate about the private ownership of guns is contentious, often nasty, and rarely insightful."[9] Debates in person or from behind a keyboard are persistent, emotional, and frustrating. It matters. People on all sides of the American gun debate understand that something real is at stake, something worth arguing over. As a nation, our gun culture reveals our values, our vision for the future, and our character. Who are we? In what way are guns a part of our identity?

Sadly, the ferocity of the American gun debate leads many to demonize or belittle their opponents. Some who carry guns even refer to themselves as "sheepdogs," heroic protectors of the cowardly sheep who refuse to protect themselves from the evil wolves.[10] The sheepdogs are the courageous good guys, intent on protecting themselves and other innocent people from the wicked. Many on the other side of the debate call them "gun lunatics" and "NRA fascists." With such sharp lines of division and heated rhetoric, the verbal and intellectual sparring shows no sign of abating.

Why is the debate about guns in the United States so contentious? Why do we scream at one another about guns? Guns have played a significant role in our nation's history, for better and for worse. America, as a modern nation, came into being in the era of the gun. In addition, the Second Amendment, the central text in the war about guns, is not clearly written: "A well regulated militia, being necessary to the security of a free state, the right of the people to keep and bear arms, shall not be infringed." The meaning of the text of this amendment can be hard to understand.

Few things spark more outrage, resentment, and anger than gun violence across ethnic groups, some incidents involving police (e.g., Michael Brown) and others involving private citizens (e.g., Trayvon Martin). Nothing creates more sadness for the family and friends of the twenty thousand people who commit suicide by gun each year.

For a variety of reasons, it often seems that more heat than light is generated by these debates. I am convinced that the status quo is unacceptable and that it can be changed.

While the gun debate rages, few books on Christian ethics address the issues in this debate. Very few books on Christian ethics or Sunday morning sermons mention, much less discuss at any length, ethical issues related to guns. Some do, and I'll consider their arguments in the pages that follow. Why this relative lack of attention to guns in Christian ethics? Perhaps other issues seem more urgent, such as abortion and the death penalty. Although these are significant topics, the role of guns in American culture is equally significant. Twenty-three people were executed by the state in 2017; in that same year, over thirty-nine thousand died by gun violence. Of course, this is not an issue of mere numbers, but the relative totals here highlight the fact that many more people die at the end of a barrel than at the hands of an executioner. Guns involve significant Christian moral issues.

A Brief History of Guns in America

For many people, guns occupy a place at the very heart of what it means to be an American. There are deep connections between guns and their way of life, with how they conceive of themselves, with their very identity. Lynyrd Skynyrd's "God and Guns" illustrates this connection well:

> God and guns
> Keep us strong
> That's what this country
> Was founded on
> Well we might as well give up and run
> If we let them take our God and guns.

For many Americans, this song expresses part of who they are. For them, guns represent or even partially constitute values such as faith, freedom, family, self-sufficiency, and patriotism. We can't tell the whole story here. Yet we can briefly explore the story of guns in America. The song above captures the story many believe. Religion, hard work, rugged independence, and guns are all part of this story. The truth is always more complicated. A fable about the past—a mythic tale of Americans and their guns—occupies the hearts and minds of many Americans.

But first the standard story, told by Pamela Haag in *The Gunning of America*:

An abridged history of the American gun culture, told from legend and popular memory, might go like this: We were born a gun culture. Americans have an exceptional, unique, and timeless relationship to guns, starting with the militias of the Revolutionary War, and it developed on its own from there. Some celebrate and some condemn this relationship, but it is in either case unique. Guns have long been a commonplace part of American life, which is why guns pretty much sell themselves. The Second Amendment, ubiquitous to contemporary gun politics, was a prominent presence historically and is a source of the gun's unique stature, while the idea of gun control is more recent. The American gun story is about civilians and individual citizens, and they are its heroes or its villains—the frontiersman, the Daniel Boone "long hunter" who trekked far into the wilderness alone, the citizen-patriot militiaman, the guiltily valorized outlaw, and the gunslinger. The gun's mystique was forged most vividly on the violent western frontier of the 1800s, and this mystique is about individualism: guns protect citizens against overzealous government infringement of liberties; they protect freedom and self-determination.[11]

Haag characterizes this story as legend and popular memory rather than fact. She argues that the existence of American gun culture is not due to the centrality of guns to our historical identity nor to some exceptional relationship that Americans have with their guns. Instead, she contends that American gun culture owes its existence to the fact that none of these claims are true.

Haag's primary point is that the current gun culture is not a product of frontier mystique, evil intent, or some form of American exceptionalism. Rather, a primary historical factor leading to the gun culture of today is, simply, business. She points out that, historically speaking, in the crucial period when guns were sold and distributed across the country by gun businesses, and subsequently for many years, a gun "was like a buckle or a pin, an unexceptional object of commerce. No pangs of conscience were attached to it . . . or mystique pertained to its manufacture, marketing, and sale."[12] Members of the gun industry, like the Winchester Repeating Arms

Company, pursued profit through the sale of guns, just as others pursued profit through manufacturing shirts, corsets, or hammers. Capitalism, not exceptionalism, drove the gun industry in the 1800s. In fact, gun businesses were at times dependent upon military contracts, both national and international, and had to create demand for their products. They could not safely assume that sufficient demand was always present. Without the international market, the gun industry in America would have likely failed. After the Civil War, many American gun industrialists failed because they had no international contracts.

As time passed, the gun industry succeeded in attaching emotional value to firearms. So, one reason Americans love guns is that the people who sold guns to them elicited that love. They did so in a variety of ways, one of which was to make the gun a rite of passage for young boys. Winchester had a marketing strategy called the "boy plan," which fostered this idea. One ad stated that "Every real American father or mother is proud these days to have a boy who can place five shots straight in the bull's eye and wear a Winchester sharpshooter medal." More tellingly, Winchester's campaign to win over parents included the claim that a gun will "make a man of any boy," teaching him the trait of self-reliance.[13] Guns were thus tied to class and masculinity.

But the barrels of America's guns did not stop there. They wrapped around and merged with other social fights and debates. David Brooks, in a *New York Times* editorial ("Guns and the Soul of America"), writes:

> A century ago, the forces of industrialization swept over agricultural America, and monetary policy became the proxy fight in that larger conflict. Today, people in agricultural and industrial America legitimately feel that their way of life is being threatened by postindustrial society. The members of this resistance have seized on issues like guns, immigration, the flag as places to mobilize their counterassault. Guns are a proxy for larger issues.

Guns are part of a cluster of issues related to an identity of many Americans, an identity they feel is under threat. The gun, Brooks says, "stands for freedom, self-reliance and the ability to control your own destiny. Gun rights are about living in a country where families are tough enough and responsible enough to stand up for themselves in a dangerous world."[14]

Without doubt, there is some truth in the American myth about guns. From the colonial period through the time of the early republic, David Yamane says, guns were the products of individual craftsmen and were needed for life on the farm and the frontier.[15] In the nineteenth century, guns became a mass-produced commodity. Additional markets needed to be created. This led to hunting becoming more than a means for getting food. Hunting with guns became a common recreational activity. In addition, target shooting became a popular sport in many places.

For most of the twentieth century, receiving a rifle was a rite of passage for many young boys, ushering them into manhood. Guns were birthday or Christmas presents. Some even found guns in their Easter baskets! The transition from the frontier to the shooting range was an important step and was followed by a more important transition: the move from recreation to armed citizenry. Yamane calls this the shift from Gun Culture 1.0 to Gun Culture 2.0.[16] Today, most gun owners cite self-defense as the primary reason for owning a gun. Gun Culture 2.0 is now the norm in the United States. Americans arm themselves to fight or prepare themselves to defend.

A large factor in this transformation is the change in concealed-carry laws that allows many more individuals to legally carry a handgun. At the end of 2011, at least eight million people had an active permit to carry a concealed handgun.[17] Jennifer Carlson reports that from 1999 to 2013, the number of Americans who carried guns for protection increased to 22 percent. In her book *Citizen-Protectors*, she examines and explains this shift. For many, "gun use and ownership represents complex responses to economic decline, social disorder, and inadequate police protection."[18] The fear of crime and a correlating distrust in the efficacy of the police motivate people to own and carry guns. In addition, economic worries and changes have made many men feel as if they can no longer assert their masculinity as providers or productive workers. Guns offer a way to do so. Finally, many feel disconnected from their communities. While many tend to think of white conservative men as exemplifying these motivations, the impact of crime, the decline in the economy, and the decline in community engagement are broader than this. Guns appeal to men of diverse backgrounds. In Michigan, one in twenty-five people has a permit, a number that holds true for both white and African American residents.[19]

The result is a model of citizenship that Carlson calls *citizen-protectors*, individuals who believe that using deadly force against others is "a morally upstanding response to a violent threat" and "view their decision to carry a gun as a commitment to this" ideal.[20] The citizen-protector sees himself as distinct from both victims and criminals; he is willing to be courageous and use lethal force to protect innocent life. Second, the citizen-protector sees a trait usually associated with police or the military—a willingness to injure or kill in protection of life—as the mark of a good citizen, not just of a good police officer or soldier. Third, the citizen-protector believes that it is better to rely on oneself and one's gun for protection than the state and the police. Some base this belief in a distrust of the police; others ground it in a desire not to be reliant upon them. But either way, this individualism, this self-reliance, is part of what it means to be a good citizen.

A study of concealed-carry license holders in Texas found that other factors also motivated individuals to own and carry handguns.[21] Males in this study were moved by the desire to protect their families. Some carried a gun to compensate for diminished physical strength due to age. Females were focused on self-protection rather than protecting their families. They also saw guns as a means of closing the gap in physical strength between them and their potential male victimizers. Both males and females embraced the value of personal responsibility.

One can conclude from the Michigan and Texas studies that a key part of Gun Culture 2.0 is that guns are more than tools of self-defense. They also carry significant symbolic value. For example, guns say something about the gun owner: "I am a law-abiding citizen and deserve to be treated with dignity" and "I'm one of the good guys."[22]

In sum, what gunned America? The gun culture that exists today is the result of different threads: pursuit of profit, life on the frontier, and self-defense. Gun manufacturers fuel interest and sell products.

The Second Amendment

The full text of the Second Amendment reads "A well regulated militia, being necessary to the security of a free state, the right of the people to keep and bear arms, shall not be infringed." Only part of this amendment is displayed prominently in the lobby of the NRA's headquarters in Fairfax, Virginia: ". . . the right of the people to keep and bear arms, shall not be infringed."

Much of the contemporary American debate focuses on this amendment, and the relationship between the clauses in it. Looking at the history of the Second Amendment reveals some of the controversial issues.

In his book *The Second Amendment: A Biography*, Michael Waldman discusses the history of this now controversial portion of the Bill of Rights.[23] The Bill of Rights was not the first such document to declare a right to bear arms.[24] The English Declaration of Rights of 1689 stated that Protestant subjects "may have arms for their defence." Waldman starts in the era of the American Revolution, then traces over two hundred years of precedent that were recently reversed by *District of Columbia v. Heller*:

> For 218 years, judges overwhelmingly concluded that the amendment authorized states to form militias, what we now call the National Guard. Then, in 2008, the U.S. Supreme Court upended two centuries of precedent. In the case of District of Columbia v. Heller, an opinion written by Justice Antonin Scalia declared that the Constitution confers a right to own a gun for self-defense in the home. That's right: the Supreme Court found there to be an individual right to gun ownership just a few years ago.[25]

Waldman examines the era of the framers of the Constitution to try to understand what they intended in the Second Amendment.

This is important but difficult to do. Determining *intent* is difficult among the living, not to mention the dead.

The debate about the intent of the framers focuses on the historical context and options for weapons when the amendment was written. During this era, gun regulations were quite common. In Boston it was illegal to keep a loaded gun in the home. Boston, along with New York and the cities of Pennsylvania, outlawed the firing of guns in city limits. People thought to be dangerous were not allowed to own weapons. Common law governed the use of guns. There was a right to self-defense, but other things were weighed against this. For instance, it was illegal to carry a weapon in a menacing manner.

With this historical context in mind, it is still difficult to determine what the framers thought the Second Amendment meant. Very little explanation is available. Many of today's gun-rights advocates contend that the English Bill of Rights, a century older than the US version, was in the minds of the framers. The English version claimed that individuals had a right to be armed and that this right was both ancient and indubitable. But there were limits even on this: it was for Protestants and upper-class Englishmen. It didn't allow all Englishmen the freedom to have a gun in their homes.

Some argue that the framers had only muskets in mind when they created the Second Amendment. It is hard to imagine that they could have plausibly imagined a fully automatic weapon. This very point was raised in a February 2018 CNN townhall meeting, soon after the Parkland school massacre.[26] Linda Schulman, whose son Scott Biegel died shielding students from gunfire during the shooting, pointed out to the NRA's Dana Loesch that "When the Second Amendment was ratified, they were talking about muskets. We're not talking about muskets. We're talking about assault rifles. We're talking about weapons of mass destruction that kill people." In reply, Loesch said that "at the time, there were fully automatic weapons that were available—the Belton gun and Puckle gun."

Loesch's reply, however, is very misleading. The Belton gun and the Puckle gun were very different from the AR-15. The Belton gun may never even have been manufactured. The Puckle gun required a crew of two to three people and could fire about 9 rounds per minute. To say the existence of these guns supports the claim that ownership of AR-15s (which can fire 90 to 180 rounds per minute) should not be limited by the Second Amendment is misguided at best. At worst, it is disingenuous and morally irresponsible.

Waldman notes that in this era militias were different from armies. Militias were made up of ordinary citizens who had a duty, rather than a right, to be armed so they could train and be ready for conflict. Armies were seen as military occupiers. The delegates of the Constitutional Convention preferred militias to a standing army for fear that Congress or the president could use the latter to control the states. The armed state militias would stand in the way of this. On whether the delegates were concerned about an individual's right to own a gun, Waldman notes that nothing in James Madison's notes—or in anyone else's—offers evidence that they thought private gun ownership was at risk and necessitated the Second Amendment: *"It simply did not come up."*[27]

According to Waldman, one reason the Second Amendment "was ignored for so long is that it is so inscrutable."[28] Rules for punctuation, spelling, and capitalization were not standardized until the next century. Moreover, the choppy grammar here is unique among the amendments. The first clause, or preamble, of the amendment—"A well regulated militia, being necessary to the security of a free state"—was the focus of the debate the framers had. Does it limit the right? Explain it? Merely introduce it? At the time, preambles were read as limiting what followed. What did "well regulated" mean? This phrase likely would not have referred to governmental control or rules but instead would have meant something like "well-disciplined" or "internally balanced," apparently referring to the desired state of the militia itself.

When we consider "the right of the people," the immediate question is, who does "people" refer to? Many today, including the Supreme Court, take it to refer to an *individual right* to a gun. Waldman argues that the framers more frequently used this to refer to the collective mass of people, the voters, or the general population.

What about "to keep and bear arms"? A search of all official debate records in the Continental and US Congresses from 1774 to 1821 yields thirty uses of the phrase "bear arms" or "bearing arms" (not including discussions of the Second Amendment). In every single case, "the phrase has an unambiguously military meaning."[29] In sum, Waldman contends: "We cannot truly know what the Framers intended. But one would have to look far to find evidence that their principal concern was the risk that government would enact gun safety laws, or disarm farmers. They may have thought widespread gun ownership obvious or necessary, but thought it equally obvious that laws could protect public safety, too."[30] This last point is crucial. As we'll see, the law of the land at present is that there is an individual legal right to own a gun. This is quite consistent, however, with conditions and limitations being placed on that right.

There are a few historically significant laws worth noting here.[31] The National Firearms Act of 1934 created a $200 tax (roughly equivalent to $3,500 today) on firearms purchased by individuals. It also required that a stamp proving the tax had been paid be affixed to the gun. Other key laws include the Gun Control Act of 1968, which made it illegal for minors, those suffering from mental illness, felons, and known drug dealers to buy or own a gun. It also set up a federal licensing system for gun dealers. In the early 1990s, the Brady Bill went into effect. It required background checks for gun purchases as well as a five-day waiting period, though these requirements were replaced in 1998 by the National Instant Criminal Background Check System. The federal ban on assault weapons also went into effect during this era, though it was allowed to expire in 2004.

The Supreme Court, in recent years, has adopted *the individual rights view*, interpreting the Second Amendment as protecting the individual right to own a gun.[32] Prior to this, the Court had taken *the collective view* of the amendment, which holds that the right to bear arms applies to communities or militias and not to each individual person. In *United States v. Miller*, the argument was that the National Firearms Act of 1934 violated the Second Amendment. Miller committed a crime with a gun that did not have the required stamp and was charged with violating the act. Miller's legal argument was that the act violated the Second Amendment right to bear arms. A lower court agreed with Miller. But the Supreme Court overruled the lower court. The Court found that the limitations of the National Firearms Act on what type of weapon an individual could possess did not violate the Second Amendment. This is because the Court held that the purpose of the amendment was to provide for a well-regulated militia. That is, it took the view that the amendment was about the collective right to bear arms for the sake of national defense.

This changed in 2008. As noted above, in *District of Columbia v. Heller*, the Court adopted the individual rights view, in a 5–4 vote. Heller challenged the ban on handguns in the District of Columbia, which had been on the books since 1975. In its decision, the Court found that the framers would have thought of the right to bear arms as a right of individuals, enabling them to protect their own lives, the lives of their families, and their property. (In 2010, the legality of a ban on handguns in Chicago and Oak Park, a Chicago suburb, was challenged in *McDonald v. City of Chicago*. The Court held that Second Amendment rights applied to the states and not just to the federal government.)[33]

I will not challenge the validity of this interpretation of the Second Amendment, though many do. While the individual rights view adopted by the Supreme Court in 2008 is the law, it is essential to keep in mind that the majority opinion explicitly states that this view is consistent with reasonable limits being placed on the right:

> Like most rights, the right secured by the Second Amendment is not unlimited. From Blackstone through the 19th-century cases, commentators and courts routinely explained that the right was not a right to keep and carry any weapon whatsoever in any manner whatsoever and for whatever purpose . . . nothing in our opinion should be taken to cast doubt on longstanding prohibitions on the possession of firearms by felons and the mentally ill, or laws forbidding the carrying of firearms in sensitive places such as schools and government buildings, or laws imposing conditions and qualifications on the commercial sale of arms.[34]

The Court, then, clearly held that different types of limitations may be placed on the right to keep and bear arms.

James Atwood describes three options for how we might interpret the Second Amendment in the years to come.[35] First, we could take the right to bear arms to be unrestricted and unregulated. On this option, no governing body could create and enact any law that puts any restrictions, conditions, or limitations on anyone owning any type of firearm. As a second option, the right to keep and bear arms can be poorly regulated. Atwood contends that this is how the amendment is applied today, and he is correct. Individuals can obtain guns from private sellers at gun shows, from other individuals, and through unethical gun dealers. The third option, which Atwood thinks is the best way of interpreting the amendment, is to

> embrace the Second Amendment our forebears actually gave us: i.e., the entire Second Amendment. All twenty seven words and both clauses . . . this is balanced and recognizes the rights of all law-abiding citizens who have clean records and are of sound mind to have guns for self-defense or recreational purposes; it also assures all citizens that intelligent, reasonable measures will be taken to regulate instruments made to kill.[36]

From a legal perspective, I agree with Atwood. The best way forward is to balance the right to bear arms with our rights to life, liberty, and the pursuit of happiness. People should be able to go to school, concerts, and their chosen house of worship without fear of being shot. While no law or set of laws will be perfect, we can do better.

With this legal history and background in mind, I will focus in the remaining chapters on the moral questions surrounding guns from a Christian perspective. For instance, is there a moral right to own a gun? And if so, what, if anything, limits the exercise of that right? I argue that there are limits on the moral right to own and use a gun, and that those limits should be reflected in the interpretation and application of the legal right.

American Christianity and Guns

Should Christians own guns? Should people carry firearms in church? Is violence against others permitted for those who seek to follow the way of Jesus? If so, when is it permissible? When is it not? What does the Bible say that is relevant to these questions?

Christians in America hold diverse views about guns and gun culture. Some Christians have never owned or fired a gun. Others appear to place the Second Amendment nearly on par with Scripture, as if appealing to it should settle the matter. In one sense, a proper interpretation and application of the Second Amendment would settle the matter *legally*. However, this would not settle the matter *morally* or *spiritually*. The mixture of faith, patriotism, and the veneration of the Constitution (the Second Amendment in particular) is worrisome. In its more extreme forms, this veneration is a perversion of the gospel and of "the faith that was once for all entrusted to the saints" (Jude 3).[37]

Consider one contemporary example: the sights on some American military weapons are engraved with references to Scripture.[38] Trijicon, a sight manufacturer, engraved on the sights "2COR4:6" and "JN8:12," two passages from the Bible. Second Corinthians 4:6 says, "For it is the God who said, 'Let light shine out of darkness,' who has shone in our hearts to give the light of the knowledge of the glory of God in the face of Jesus Christ." John 8:12 states, "Again Jesus spoke to them, saying, 'I am the light of the world. Whoever follows me will never walk in darkness but will have the light of life.'" This combination of a Bible and a gun is very troubling for a variety of reasons, including the fact that there is no sound interpretation of these verses that makes their use appropriate. Moreover, there are other reasons that this is simply wrong. It arguably violates the Constitution, and it fosters the view among many that American involvement in the Middle East is a crusade. From a Christian perspective, it supports the false view that God is on America's side. Further, it neglects the fact that all human beings are made in God's image. It also makes the terrible mistake of associating the light of Christ with the flash of a muzzle.

This distortion of the faith exemplifies some aspects of Christian nationalism, which is an extreme form of right-wing American Christian ideology. Christian nationalism includes several core beliefs, such as (1) the Bible should be the only foundation for all of American life; (2) the United States must be returned to its status as a Christian nation; (3) conservative Christians are superior and have a right to rule over America; and (4) Christians must keep our nation from its continuing slide into the corruption wrought by secular humanism.[39] There are many problems inherent in this ideology. First, Christians should not seek to build a Christian state, but rather a just state. Second, Christian nationalism is both morally reprehensible and theologically unsound. The idea that conservative Christians are superior is ludicrous, as is the related Christian nationalist belief that they have a right to rule the United States because Genesis 1:28 gives them dominion over all the earth. Among the clearest teachings of the Bible is that followers of Christ are not to consider themselves superior to *anyone*. The example of Jesus as described by Paul in Philippians 2:5-11 should undermine any such attitude of superiority. And Genesis 1:28 has nothing to do with who has a right to govern the United States.

How is Christian nationalism relevant to thinking about God and guns in America? Some of the tendencies associated with Christian nationalism are also evident among some conservative Christians, such as: the tendency to exhibit fear because they perceive the world a dangerous place; ethnocentrism; nationalism; support for weakening Constitutional protections of liberty (except the Second Amendment) and, related to this, the tendency to oppose gun-control legislation.[40] I am not claiming that Christians who are not Christian nationalists but oppose more gun-control legislation are guilty by association. Rather, my point is that some of the tendencies of Christian nationalists are also present in mainstream conservative Christianity. And this is very troubling. For example, most, if not all, Christian nationalists believe that the United States is better than any other country in the history of the world. Many think the United States is like a modern-day Israel, a nation with a special relationship to God that is uniquely blessed by God for the good of all other nations. And some also possess racist beliefs and defend racist speech. Given that many Christian nationalist beliefs are immoral and irrational, the fact that some of their other beliefs have become more mainstream reinforces the point that those beliefs should be subjected to strict scrutiny. The mix of nationalism, fear of danger, suspicion of the other, and opposition to restrictions on who can own or use a gun plays a role in thought about God and guns in America, and the policies that many conservative Christians support.

For example, after the mass shooting in San Bernardino, Jerry Falwell Jr., president of Liberty University, announced during a convocation that all students would be able to take a free concealed-carry class. Falwell's solution to San Bernardino is *the-good-guy-with-a-gun solution*: "If more good people had concealed-carry permits, then we could end those Muslims before they walked in and killed them." He went on to encourage Liberty students to "teach them a lesson if they ever show up here."[41] Falwell is not alone among Christian leaders. Gary Cass, a pastor in Texas, speaking at a church conference entitled "Deliver Us from Evil: Declaring War on the Devil's War against America," told attendees that they have not only the right but also the responsibility to own a firearm. Cass claimed that "You can't be a Christian if you don't own a gun." Another Texas pastor, James McAbee, believes that "it's very important that every church, pastor and all, have a gun." It is not just fear of criminals that motivates such attitudes toward guns but also fear of the government. Dallas area pastor Stephen Broden, during a protest of a gun buyback, said that "The moment they disarm us, we move in the direction of a tyrannical government who will rob us of our liberties."[42]

Falwell, Cass, McAbee, Broden, and others might be dismissed as outside the mainstream of conservative Christian thought. But I'm not sure such a dismissal is warranted. Many American Christians who are not fully Christian nationalists hold such views on God and guns. These Christians also oppose more restrictive gun legislation, but they do not share many of the immoral beliefs and tendencies of Christian nationalism. They are saddened and angered by gun violence but remain strong supporters of the Second Amendment and are opposed to putting more laws on the books.

Other Christians, however, are intent on challenging the status quo about guns in this country. John Piper, for example, responded to Falwell, expressing his concern about "the forging of a disposition in Christians to use lethal force, not as policemen or soldiers, but as ordinary Christians in relation to harmful adversaries."[43] In reply to a mind-set like that of Falwell, who carries a gun and encourages students to do the same, Piper argues that an attitude of "Don't mess with me, I have the power to kill you in my pocket" is inconsistent with the teachings of the New Testament. Christians, he contends, should accept unjust treatment and not retaliate; we should not seek to advance the cause of Christ with a weapon; we are to patiently endure suffering rather than resist it with arms; and, finally, our lives should lead people to ask us about our hope in and reliance on God, not our guns.

Rob Schenck, another Christian with a history of pro-life activism, has turned his attention in recent years to evangelicalism and guns. His journey on this issue is the focus of the documentary film *The Armor of Light*. He discusses the documentary and his views on guns in his book *Costly Grace*.[44] For years Schenck just assumed that supporting Second Amendment rights was a given. But, for a variety of reasons, he began to experience "a creeping discomfort with what appeared to be my community's growing infatuation with deadly force."[45] He was hesitant to discuss his changing views on gun control on camera. He was worried that this would likely severely damage his personal and professional relationships. The problem was, "Gun rights were part and parcel of social policy that had been assembled by a coalition of conservative forces for over almost forty years. To publicly question the Second Amendment could more quickly lead to my being branded a traitor than if I questioned a core article of the Christian faith. . . . Guns could be the cause of my professional suicide."[46] But Schenck could not escape his growing conviction that there was a contradiction among many conservative evangelicals. On one hand they are strongly pro-life, but on the other hand they love guns and are adamantly opposed to gun control.

Still other Christians, across the political spectrum, are pacifists. They reject violence and so choose never to own a gun or to fire one at another human being. For example, Bruce Reyes-Chow, former pastor and now a teaching elder in the Presbyterian Church (USA), chooses not to own a gun for a number of reasons. His place in the greater community leads him to forgo owning a gun. Not owning a gun prevents him or others from using that gun to commit an act of violence. Also, in the Scriptures Jesus never gives his followers permission to solve their problems through violence, even in response to violence. Christians, according to Reyes-Chow, must stand together and "let the world know that there is a different way to live and respond to that which may threaten us . . . *and it is one that does not involve guns.*"[47]

For these and other reasons, Christian activist Shaine Claiborne has been applying the vision of God's kingdom from the book of Isaiah—where swords are beaten into plowshares—by literally turning guns into garden tools:

> There is something special about seeing the transformation happen before your eyes, and hearing the sound of the forge and the pounding of the metal, something therapeutic about taking a hammer to the barrel of a gun. A few months back, we did another LIVE weapon-conversion, turning a fully operative AK47 into three hand trowels in front of thousands of folks at the Justice Conference. Now we use one of the hand trowels from that AK47 in our garden here in Philadelphia . . . where we tragically see nearly one gun death per day. It just feels good for the soul each time we beat a gun into oblivion . . . it feels like the world is a better place with one less semi-automatic.[48]

Christians in America are a very diverse group when it comes to guns. Some celebrate them. Others accept them as necessary in a fallen world. Others worry about their impact on society and our souls. And others, out of a principled pacifism, choose to turn them into garden tools, seeking to manifest the promised future peace in our present fallen world.

Conclusion

The sentiments of many resonate with the words in Lynyrd Skynyrd's "God and Guns." Others, however, are compelled by the images in Mark Erelli's song "By Degrees":

I've seen little hands on little shoulders
Children in a line
I've seen them led away from school
As the shots rang out inside
And I thought something had to change
But somehow it's become routine
We can learn to live with anything
When it happens by degrees.[49]

Should Christians side with Lynyrd Skynyrd or Mark Erelli? Is our country founded on God and guns? Have we become desensitized to gun violence by degrees? More central to our purposes here, is there one correct Christian view about gun violence, gun rights, and gun control? These are controversial and difficult issues. I believe God does have a view about these things. But I also recognize that there is room for disagreement among thoughtful, committed Christians on these issues. In the pages that follow, my goal is to offer one particular Christian perspective on God and guns in America. I think the view I explain and defend is true, and I hope it engenders reflection and even social and political change, as needed.

The perspective I explain and defend in this book seeks to challenge the status quo. Gun violence does not need to be normal. Think about the most recent mass shooting in America. It doesn't have to be this way. Christians must not normalize gun violence, letting our views be shaped by particular political ideologies rather than Scripture, reason, and other sources of truth. Christians are not obligated to own a gun, and we should not accept weapons during our worship services as easily as many would have us do.

For many, God and guns are like hot dogs and apple pie. They are part of what it means to be an American, and even an American Christian. The problem is that this combination of faith and firearms is often accepted for dubious reasons and can lead to disastrous consequences.

2

THE RIGHT TO OWN A GUN

In Charlton Heston's speech at the annual meeting of the NRA in 2000, he said that "sacred stuff resides in that wooden stock and blued steel—something that gives the most common man the most uncommon of freedoms." He concluded the speech with the famous words, that any who would strip him of his right to own a gun must do so "from my cold, dead hands."[1]

Heston's words reveal a belief that the right to own and use a gun is not merely a legal right, granted by the Constitution, but a right given by God. Understood this way, the right to own a gun is not just a *legal* right but a *moral* right. One need not believe in God to believe that this is a moral right—people talk of human rights or natural rights in the context of moral rights. The point is that the existence of such a right does not depend on the law. Rather, a moral right exists whether or not it is recognized by the law.

The Nature of Rights

A few years ago I was a guest on a radio program, Up for Debate, with David Barton. We were debating whether Christians should support gun control. In the discussion, Barton claimed that the right to own a gun is inalienable. He appealed to the Second Amendment as a God-given right that cannot be forfeited. At the time, I was shocked by this claim. I continue to be. If I have a right to something, then others are obligated at least to avoid interfering with what that right protects. For a right to be inalienable, it cannot be lost or surrendered. Inalienable means "incapable of being alienated, surrendered, or transferred." However, few rights are truly inalienable. In the case of guns, we expect that the right to bear arms does not apply to the criminally insane or those who pose a demonstrable, immediate danger to themselves or others. We suspend or revoke rights in those cases, for the good of the person and the good of society. It's common sense.

Many current debates about controversial issues make use of the language of rights. We argue about the right to choose, the right to life, the right to die, the right to privacy, parental rights, and so on. In the gun debates, claims about the right to own a gun are often pitted against claims about the right to life of victims of gun violence. However, there is some confusion about the nature of rights.

First, there is an important distinction between a legal right and a moral right.[2] A *legal right* is stated within a particular law or legal code. A legal right does not exist unless it is present in a legal code. For example, the Voting Rights Act of 1965 is intended to secure the right to vote for everyone, regardless of race. The Voting Rights Act prohibits racial discrimination in voting. In this case, the legal right recognizes a *moral right* that already existed, the right of all citizens not to be discriminated against by having their voting rights denied.

A *moral right* is possessed by an individual whether or not it is recognized by the law. For example, in the era of apartheid, the black majority did not possess many important legal rights in South Africa. A key argument against apartheid was that it failed to recognize that such discrimination was immoral. Apartheid failed to recognize the moral right to nondiscrimination. As such, fundamental moral rights were being violated, and the ending of apartheid was brought about when these rights were recognized and protected by the law.

In our country, given the *Heller* and *McDonald* cases, individuals at present clearly have a legal right to own a gun. One might argue about whether this is the correct legal view, but one cannot argue that no such legal right exists. Americans have a *legal right* to own a gun. The deeper question, however, is whether there is a *moral right* to own a gun. Not all legal rights are moral and not all moral rights are legal. And if there is a moral right, what is the nature and extent of that right?

Most rights are *conditional*, that is, one must meet certain conditions to possess and exercise a right. If not, one forfeits that right. Such a right can be overridden by the rights of others. An *absolute* or inalienable right cannot be forfeited and cannot be overridden. Whether any absolute or inalienable rights exist is controversial. Some argue that all people have a right not to be tortured, whereas others argue that this can be forfeited in some situations. Many believe that the right to life is an absolute right, whereas others think it can be forfeited by those who commit murder.

All the moral rights that are also recognized as legal rights in the United States have limits. The Supreme Court affirms that no Constitutional right is absolute. Nevertheless, some proponents of gun rights contend that the right to own a gun cannot be limited by the government. But they are mistaken. None of our other rights work that way.[3] When good reasons for limiting a right exist, the government has the power to do so. We cannot use our right to freedom of speech to incite murder, cause a riot, or say any word we choose on television. Neither can we use religion to justify certain forms of discrimination. Similar considerations come into play with gun rights. In fact, many limits are already in place. People can be prohibited from owning a machine gun or a rocket-propelled grenade. As noted above, felons and people with certain mental illnesses are prohibited from owning firearms. Children are as well.

Usually, rights are limited to prevent harm and unintended consequences. It is illegal and immoral to yell "Fire!" in a crowded theater when there is no fire. The resulting chaos could lead to injury or death. If your religion requires it, you cannot sacrifice a university professor to satisfy the wrath of your gods. The rights described as legal rights in the First Amendment are limited by significant harm to others. So are the rights in the Second Amendment, in both their legal and moral forms.

In sum, the following distinctions about rights will be useful to keep in mind:

Legal right: a right that is stated within a law or legal code.

Moral right: a right that one has whether or not it is recognized by law. This type of right may come from God or nature, or simply be a feature of moral reality.

Absolute right: a right that one cannot forfeit; it cannot be overridden.

Conditional right: a right that can be forfeited when one fails to demonstrate the relevant abilities for responsibly exercising it; it can be overridden by the rights of others.

The Right to Life and the Right to Own a Gun

The right to life is the most important right. It is recognized in various constitutions, legal systems, religions, philosophies, and the United Nations Universal Declaration of Human Rights. All human beings possess this fundamental moral right.

Some argue that the moral right to own a gun, as a potential means of self-defense, is grounded in the right to life. As advocates for gun rights point out, a firearm can be a very effective means of self-defense and can be useful for securing one's own right to life. The mere presence of a gun can deter criminals from committing their intended crime. Even if a criminal is unarmed, the criminal may have a large size or strength advantage. In such cases, a gun in the hands of a potential victim can tip the scales back in his or her favor. If an aggressor is threatening my life or the life of someone else, a case can be made that a gun is an important, and sometimes the most effective, means of defense. Given this, the right to own a gun could be grounded in the right to self-defense, which is grounded in the right to life.[4]

But is there a right to kill another person to defend one's own life or the life of someone else? Many believe so. One common way of arguing for this claim has to do with the idea that a person can forfeit his rights. For example, if I steal from my neighbor, it seems like I forfeit some of my own rights. The state has the right to confiscate some of my property to provide restitution to my neighbor.

If the theft warrants it, the state may even incarcerate me. In these situations, I forfeit some of my property rights or my liberty rights. Similarly, some argue that if a person is attempting to murder another person (and thus violating her right to life), then the offender forfeits his own right to life. In such a case, the victim is morally justified in taking the life of the offender.

But how would this give a potential victim a right to own and use a gun? The individual right to life entitles individuals to use whatever reasonable means are needed to protect that right. It would make little sense, morally speaking, to argue that someone has the right to life but not the right to reasonable means to defend that right. So a person's right to life, or the right to life of another that he will protect, entails that he also has a right to the means (within reason) to secure that right. If one person is trying to harm another person, the potential victim has a right to use the means to stop the violence. Put simply, if a gun is needed for securing someone's right to life, then we may be able to derive the right to own and use a gun from the right to life.[5]

While a gun is not always *necessary* for defending life, in many cases it is. This may be enough to ground the moral right to own a gun. In cases where a gun is not needed, it may not be morally permissible to use one. Moreover, in the future, if we develop effective nonlethal technology for self-defense and defense of others, then this could make the right to own a gun, for these purposes, obsolete.

This is the strongest argument for the moral right to own and use a gun: defense of oneself or others. But even if we accept the argument, it does not follow that the status quo regarding gun laws is acceptable. Whether or not stricter gun laws are needed remains an open question. Even the right to self-defense is not absolute. Nor is the obligation to protect others from harm. For example, no individual should be able to own weapons of mass destruction claiming that defending herself or himself from a possible future attack from another person or government might require it. If my neighbor claimed the right to own a small nuclear device in order to deter some future tyrannical government from acting against him, he would be wrong. *Legally*, a citizen of the United States does not have the right to own a functioning nuclear weapon. The point here is that even the right to self-defense has limits, related to the possible serious harm that may come to innocent people. Given this, it follows that the moral right to own a gun has limits as well. It can be forfeited. It can be overridden. It is a conditional right.

The moral right to own a gun can, in some cases, be overridden by other rights.[6] For example, innocent people have the right not to be shot; this is grounded in their right not to be assaulted or killed. This right not to be shot must be enforced. Enforcing it "includes taking reasonable measures to prevent innocent people from being shot. . . . Gun control is compatible with gun ownership rights and merely limits the scope of gun rights by reasonably enforcing the right not to be shot."[7] The right not to be shot should be reflected in the law. When considering possible limits on the right to own a gun, all these rights must be taken into account: the right to own a gun, the right to self-defense, the right not to be shot, and the right to a reasonably safe environment.

Recreation and the Right to Own a Gun

A moral right to own a gun may encompass other reasons as well. For many people, owning and using a gun is a central part of their lives.[8] The recreational value is often ignored in our national debates on these issues, but it shouldn't be. Of course, recreation is not as important as life and death, but it is an important thing that gives value to our lives.

Many gun enthusiasts enjoy target shooting, hunting, or participating in shooting competitions. Shooting and hunting can forge friendships. My dad, for example, has owned and used guns my entire life. He's very competitive in shotgun sports (trap, skeet, and sporting clays), winning several awards over the years. One of the joys of retired life for him is the extra time to shoot with friends and participate in various competitions. He has a true passion for shooting sports and hunting. If laws were enacted that prevented him from doing this, his quality of life would suffer. In many ways, shooting is part of a way of life for him. It's not the most important thing in his life, of course, but it is very significant.

Many proponents of strict gun laws fail to understand or appreciate the joy of a gun. This is a mistake. We should not discount something that has such value for others simply because it does not have that same value for us. Think about your own favorite hobby or recreational pursuit. Then imagine that because others use the tools of that hobby to harm people, people want to ban the hobby altogether. This is how many gun enthusiasts currently feel. They wonder why they, as responsible gun owners, should sacrifice something they love because of the actions of others who are irresponsible and immoral.

However, recreational gun use has limits. The right is not absolute and inalienable. Harm, or potential harm to others, trumps my recreational use of a weapon. For example, someone may want to race his car with his friends on the interstate, but the risk of harm to others means that he does not have a right to do so. There are limits on the speed at which he can drive. Similarly, someone may want to own anthrax, but the risk of harm to others overrides any alleged right to do so. Nevertheless, there are reasons, apart from self-defense or defending others, that support the claim of a conditional moral right to own and use a gun. This should be considered as we craft gun laws and policies.

The responsibilities of those who would own and use guns must also be considered. Our rights do not exist in a vacuum. They must be exercised in a morally responsible manner.

Rights, Responsibilities, and Stand-Your-Ground Laws

With rights come responsibilities. This is true of many of the significant moral rights that are recognized as legal rights by the Constitution. The rights to freedom of speech, freedom of the press, and freedom of religion are conditional rights. One must meet certain conditions to exercise these rights, and they can be forfeited if one fails to do so. They can also be overridden by the rights of others. This is also true of the right to own and use a gun.

As discussed above, there are limits on even very important rights. Consider speech. Laws regulate and punish certain types of speech: slander and libel. In the United States, someone found guilty of such speech acts can be made to pay financial damages to the offended party.

Responsibilities are connected to the rights that other people have. As some like to say, "Your right to swing your arm ends where my nose begins." Your rights, your liberties, are limited when they begin to impinge on my own. Similarly, then, the right to own a gun is limited when the exercise of that liberty threatens the rights of others.

All human beings possess at least two moral rights: the right to live in security, and the right to live in freedom. The right to live in security includes the right not to be shot, discussed above. The right to live in freedom and security includes the right to a reasonably safe environment. These rights are relevant to both those who choose to own a gun and those who do not. How so?

Those who want to own a gun arguably have the right to do so and should be free to exercise that right. The right to live in security is often given as a justification for this, as well as the right to freely choose to do so. This makes sense and is important. However, it does not justify current American practice. This is because other members of society have these same rights, which limit who has the right to own a gun, what types of guns can be owned, and how those who own a gun use it.

For example, the right to live in security means that students have the right to go to school without fear of being shot. We are invasively screened before boarding airplanes. People have a right to go to work, the movies, a sporting event, or for a walk without fear. They should be free to do such things without being shot. People who are suicidal have a right to security as well. Yet, most people believe it should be more difficult for them to gain access to a firearm to protect them from making a rash and irreversible decision.

Limits on gun ownership are also justified by the rights to freedom and security that all of us possess. Thus, we prevent certain classes of people from legally obtaining weapons. Dangerous and incompetent people with guns endanger the rights of others to security and freedom. Unfettered access to guns, lax laws, and the lax enforcement of laws threaten these rights to security and freedom.

We need to balance the right to own a gun with other rights that are in play. We can do this without banning all guns *and* without accepting the status quo. We hear a lot about the right to own a gun, but we need to craft laws and foster a culture that emphasizes the responsibilities that come with that right and the importance of recognizing *all* the rights of others. Those who cannot fulfill the responsibilities should not have the right.

Those who would use a gun to defend their own life or others' lives have another key responsibility. That is the moral obligation to do so only *as a last resort*. There should be a strong presumption against the use of a firearm, because lives are at stake, for the guilty and the innocent. The use of a gun in a particular case should be reasonable, given the nature of the aggression and the specific circumstances. It is difficult to spell out a complete list of principles to follow here, given the wide variety of possible circumstances. But this does raise important issues related to stand-your-ground laws.

Stand-your-ground laws are supposed to protect the right of individuals to use lethal force in self-defense not only in the home but also in any place they are legally allowed to be. They are also intended to allow individuals to use such force in defense of their property. The standard for the right to use such force is "when one experiences what a 'reasonable person' would consider a threat, even if the person could safely retreat from the perceived danger."[9] It is not always clear when one is truly in danger. Many people fear others, but the fear of others and the belief that one's life is at risk are often unreasonable. Some critics argue that merely *feeling* threatened can be enough for justifying lethal actions under these laws. This is an unreasonable, incomplete, and often unjust standard.

Take one example: the Florida stand-your-ground law, which focuses on belief rather than feeling:

> A person is justified in using or threatening to use deadly force if he or she reasonably believes that using or threatening to use such force is necessary to prevent imminent death or great bodily harm to himself or herself or another or to prevent the imminent commission of a forcible felony. A person who uses or threatens to use deadly force in accordance with this subsection

does not have a duty to retreat and has the right to stand his or her ground if the person using or threatening to use the deadly force is not engaged in a criminal activity and is in a place where he or she has a right to be.[10]

But an important problem arises here, even if we focus on a reasonable belief standard. The presumed reasonableness of perceptions of danger is often the product of bias or prejudice, including racial bias or prejudice. Whites who kill blacks are eleven times more likely to be found innocent of a crime in states with stand-your-ground laws than blacks who kill whites. The rationalizations for the killings of Tamir Rice, Trayvon Martin, Jordan Davis—and we can add Philando Castile, Stephon Clark, and Walter Scott—reveal "a common thread: our legal structures and agents deemed it reasonable to perceive (unarmed) Black people as threatening."[11]

It is sometimes difficult to ascertain what really happened in such instances, and whether the person standing his or her ground was acting reasonably. This is because in many cases the only other eyewitness is dead. As Ta-Nehisi Coates observes,

> What we have in Florida—and doubtlessly in other parts of the country—is the state relinquishing a crucial aspect of meting out justice. The logic here militates toward getting a gun—even for people who don't like guns. The logic incentivizes an armed citizenry where the beneficiary of justice is simply the last man standing. Your side of the story is irrelevant if you are dead.[12]

Of course, not all people are at the mercy of racial bias and prejudice in these situations. Many within the judicial, legal, and law enforcement communities do not deem "it reasonable to perceive (unarmed) Black people as threatening." Nevertheless, it is clear that widespread problems exist, and that stand-your-ground laws are susceptible to and are in part born out of prejudice. This means that many people are not using firearms as a last resort, in the applicable sense. This is a moral failure, a failure to fulfill their responsibilities in this realm of life.

Morally speaking, then, in order to exercise one's right to own a gun, it is obvious that one must be able to do so in a morally responsible manner. Given the stakes, our laws and how they are enforced should reflect this. If one cannot exercise this right in a responsible manner, that right should be forfeit.

Conclusion

Moving forward, I will assume that there is a reasonable moral right to own a gun and that this right should be reflected in the law. I will also assume that this is entirely consistent with the placement of legal limits on who can own and use a gun—as well as what types of guns can be owned and used—for the purpose of defending life. In addition, I'll assume that only those who are able to exercise this right in a responsible manner should possess the right.

3

GUNS, LIES, AND BAD ARGUMENTS

Most conversations in America about guns are entertaining or frustrating, but they are rarely informative. False claims are presented. Bad arguments are advanced. Family, friends, and strangers use social media (especially Facebook) to promote their positions. Free to think; free to publish. Sound bites function as arguments. Memes masquerade as logic. People dig in. Their positions rarely change. The time and effort exerted seem to yield little gain.

In this chapter we'll examine some of the more popular arguments about guns. We will focus on the more prominent false claims and bad arguments. False claims distort reality, past and present. Bad arguments involve logical fallacies.[1] An argument contains a logical fallacy when it contains a fatal mistake in reasoning. Unfortunately, logical fallacies are common. They can also be persuasive.

One common fallacy in the gun debates is the hasty generalization. For example, I might argue that since three members of the NRA are irresponsible gun owners, it follows that most NRA members are irresponsible gun owners. But those three members do not represent the whole. Three people are insufficient. A larger sample is surely needed to make any such general claim. Or I may argue that the city of Chicago has a high rate of gun violence and then point out that it has very strict gun laws. If I conclude from this that stricter gun laws do not work, I've made a logical error. Surely, we need more evidence than one city gives us to draw such a conclusion. Both of these lines of reasoning are examples of a hasty generalization.

It would be nice if all bad arguments were as easy to detect as these two examples, and if we could always easily see what is false and what is true in the gun debate. But they aren't, and we can't. In fact, what makes some false claims and bad arguments so attractive and even convincing to many is that they often possess *some* truth. This gives them the appearance of being valid points or good arguments.

Further complicating discussions about guns, we are more apt to make errors in reasoning when an issue is important to us and generates strong emotions. Debates about guns in America touch on issues of great importance: life and death, constitutional rights, and beliefs about God, patriotism, liberty, safety, and security. As a result, conversations turn into debates and debates turn into arguments. Lots of words and lots of emotions! Few facts and few good arguments.

In the pages that follow, I will briefly introduce and address ten common claims in America's gun debates. People on both sides of the debate make false claims and give bad arguments.

1. "Violence Is on the Rise in America"

The twenty-four-hour news cycle can make it seem like violence, and gun violence in particular, is on the rise in the United States. Fortunately, this is simply not true. There was a persistent high rate of violence in America that began in 1963 and lasted for thirty years. However, the current overall homicide rate is similar to the levels of the 1950s. For example, in 2011 the overall homicide rate and the gun homicide rate were about half of the rates in 1991.

One could attribute this drop in gun homicides to improved treatment of gunshot victims. It's likely that many gunshot victims who would have died in the past are now being saved due to increased knowledge gained about treating such victims in Vietnam, Iraq, and Afghanistan, as well as within our borders. Although possible, this is not the best explanation. As others have pointed out, all forms of criminal violence have been declining since the 1990s, not just gun violence.

However, suicides involving a firearm show less of a decline. In 1990, guns were used in 61 percent of suicides. In 2010, that rate dropped by 10 percent. This decline corresponds with the decline in the number of homes in which a gun is present. We'll return to this issue below.

The false claim that violence, especially gun violence, is on the rise, may in part be caused by the ever-present stream of media as compared to even fifteen years ago. Another reason is that mass shootings generate a large amount of media attention. The number of these shootings that happen at places like schools, workplaces, and movie theaters *has risen* in the past decade or so. These recurring tragedies shake us for a variety of reasons, and sustained antigun activism that emerges from school shootings, in particular, keeps gun homicide in the front of our minds. Schools, of all places, should be safe.

If violence and gun violence are not in fact on the rise in America, what impact does that have on our conversations about guns? First, whatever positions we defend on these issues must not be based on the false belief that gun violence is at historically high levels. We need to ground our arguments and our policies in fact. Second, guns do play other roles, beyond homicide, in violent crime. The evidence shows that when guns are involved in acts of violence, the level of violence and degree of injury intensify.[2] For example, when a gun is used in a robbery or assault, it is more likely that the victim will die compared to similar crimes in which a different weapon is used. In domestic violence cases, the victim is much more likely to die if a gun is available. This is not explained by the intent of the attacker, as one might expect. If one intends to kill someone else, then one would likely choose a gun to do so. If no gun is available, the attacker would find another means to accomplish his goal. But evidence reveals that the type of weapon does matter. That is, in cases where a gun is involved, even compared to cases of multiple stabbings, death is more likely. Although violence and gun violence in particular are statistically down, the presence of a gun in a conflict situation increases the likelihood of death and serious injury.

Guns intensify violence in suicides as well. Suicide attempts using a firearm are much more effective. When a gun is used in a suicide attempt, death is the result over 80 percent of the time.[3] Those who are determined to commit suicide, if that determination persists, will likely find another means to do so. The majority of decisions to attempt suicide, however, are made in response to temporary circumstances. For example, teen suicides are very impulsive. If a gun is easily accessible, the impulse can be quickly carried out. The availability of a gun means that this impulsive decision will be more likely to end in death. Research about firearms and suicide reveals, first, compared to other high-income countries, that the rate of suicide in America is somewhere in the middle.[4] But for younger people, the mortality rate is 1.6 times higher than average, mainly because the rate of suicide by firearms is 8 times higher than the average for such countries. In addition, suicide rates are higher in rural areas than in urban ones, and guns are used more frequently in suicide attempts there. Where guns are more prevalent, both overall suicide rates and rates where a gun is used are higher. This is true even when risk factors such as psychological health, the use and abuse of alcohol and drugs, education, poverty, and unemployment are taken into account.

Some challenge the view that the presence and accessibility of a gun in the home contribute to suicides, because it could be that people in households with firearms happen to be more suicidal. Perhaps suicidal people buy guns in order to commit suicide, which would explain the data without leading to the conclusion that it is guns that impose a risk (this is referred to as "reverse causation"). In response, Matthew Miller, Deborah Azrael, and David Hemenway point out that studies reveal no higher level of suicide risk factors in households with guns. They also argue that "It is very unlikely . . . that the strong association between firearms and suicide reported consistently in U.S. studies is either spurious or substantially overrated. . . . Individual-level studies have often controlled for measures of psychopathology."[5] And in reply to claims about reverse causation, they point out that the suicide risk applies to all members of households where guns are present, not just to the owner of the gun. "A gun in the home increases the likelihood that a family member will die from suicide."[6]

Contrary to common assumptions, violence, violent crime, and suicide are not on the rise in America. Yet they remain serious problems. Firearms are involved in the deaths of thousands of people every year, due to criminal acts, suicide, or accidents.

2. "Violence Never Solves Anything"

It is true that violence can and often does beget more violence, and that we all too often resort to violence when it is not necessary to do so. However, it is false that violence never solves anything. As David Kopel puts it, the claim that violence never solves anything "is the ethical equivalent of flat-earth geography. It is a purportedly empirical claim that is contradicted by ample and obvious evidence."[7]

Kopel gives several examples of successful violence. Police and the good that they do serve as one such example. Law enforcement officers have prevented much violence, or the exacerbation of further violence, with both the threat and use of physical force. In some instances law enforcement wrongly employs violence, targeting people due to race, for example. There is no excuse for this, and justice cries out for the cessation of these immoral attitudes and actions. But acknowledging immoral examples of the use of force does not undermine the claim that there are other proper uses of it by the police.

Violence also helped to free the slaves in the American South, prevented Napoleon from gaining power over all of Europe, ended the Holocaust, toppled a Communist dictatorship in Romania, and prevented United Airlines flight 93 from killing innocents in Washington, DC, on September 11, 2001. Kopel admits that nonviolence is sometimes more effective than violence. There are cases in which violence and nonviolence are most effective when used together as the means to a just end. Violence can serve the end of justice in an effective manner.

People who are not members of law enforcement or the military have used firearms to prevent the loss of innocent life. For example, in 2007 a gunman killed two people and injured three more at the New Life Church in Colorado Springs before former police officer

Jeanne Assam, who was a volunteer security officer at the church, confronted and killed him. In 2010, sixty-nine-year-old Ethel Jones wounded a burglar at her Alabama home with a handgun. In 2012, Sarah McKinley, a young mother who had recently lost her husband to cancer, shot and killed an intruder who was armed with a knife. In 2013, a person opened fire at a middle school in Atlanta. An armed security guard was able to disarm the shooter. Only one student was wounded, and none were killed. In 2018, a gunman opened fire at a McDonald's in Birmingham, Alabama. Two employees heard the shots and hid in the freezer. A customer who was leaving with his two sons was carrying a gun. He drew and shot the gunman, who later died. The customer and one of his sons were injured, but their injuries were not life threatening. An employee who hid in the freezer said of the customer who saved his life, "He's my hero. Because I can only imagine how it would've went if he wasn't armed."[8]

Firearms are used in self-protective behaviors in response to an attempted or actual violent crime approximately 58,500 times per year.[9] Violence is not always the answer, and we resort to it much more often than we should. Nevertheless, it can sometimes save lives and prevent other injustices from occurring.

3. "The NRA Is to Blame"

A familiar refrain after a mass shooting is that the National Rifle Association is to blame; it has the blood of innocent people on its hands. After the Parkland school shooting, celebrities like Chelsea Handler and public figures like Hillary Clinton laid at least some of the blame at the feet of the NRA. Critics blame the NRA for such deaths because it opposes any new restrictions on gun ownership and use, supports removing restrictions that are in place, and donates large sums of money to political candidates who then stick to the NRA party line. Defenders of the NRA reply that it is a civil rights organization, protecting the Second Amendment rights of every American citizen. Many gun-rights supporters believe that more guns will make us safer. This belief undergirds much of the political action of the NRA. It also provides motivation for purchasing more and more firearms.

But is the NRA to blame? In some senses that answer is clearly no. In other ways the answer is yes. To see why, consider some facts about the organization and its activities.[10] There are three distinct organizations within the NRA. There is the organization, made up of several million members, that engages in political advocacy for gun rights. There is also a charitable foundation, which is active in providing grants to gun clubs and develops gun-safety programs for use across the country. The third organization is a political action committee (PAC) that donates money to political candidates. This last group, the PAC, spent roughly $16 million during the 2012 elections.

This last point is important, and helps us to see one sense in which the NRA is not to blame.[11] The oft-repeated story that the NRA wields power over policy makers through large donations, thereby preventing them from voting for stricter gun laws, is misleading. In fact, the NRA spends less on lobbying efforts than some other groups. Since 1998, the NRA has spent $203 million in the political realm, most of which goes to issue-focused television commercials, not to individual candidates. Compare this to the $1.1 billion spent by the financial industry in the 2016 election cycle alone. Taking 2012 as a starting point, the majority of the members of Congress have not received money from the NRA. Many candidates already share the perspective of the NRA on these issues. They are not being forced to do so by large campaign contributions. Even Marco Rubio, who has come under much criticism for taking money from the NRA, receives relatively little from them compared to all the donations he receives. Since 2009, the NRA accounts for 3.3 percent of his donations. There have been cases in which proposed legal and policy changes with respect to guns and the mentally ill or people on the no-fly list of the Transportation Security Administration (TSA) were opposed by both the NRA and the American Civil Liberties Union (ACLU). It was the NRA in conjunction with the ACLU and others that influenced policy in these instances.

But the case can also be made that the NRA shares the blame for some of the injuries and deaths that occur via firearms in America.

Cook and Goss note that surveys in Washington, DC, show that political types believe it is one of the most powerful special interest groups active in the capital.[12] It is the ability of the NRA to mobilize its members, rather than the money it spends on elections, that lies at the heart of its power to influence public policy. The dues of millions of members help fund grassroots lobbying at the local, state, and national levels.

The NRA has helped produce the gun laws that currently exist in America in several ways.[13] It has been instrumental in preventing the reinstatement of the federal assault weapons ban that was in existence from 1994 to 2004. It helped prevent government funding for research on the public health effects of firearms. It helped get a federal law passed in 2005 that immunizes those who manufacture, distribute, and sell guns from many types of lawsuits. The NRA and its affiliates have successfully worked to deregulate firearms at the state level. Some also contend that the NRA protects the firearms industry from criticism and political pressure when mass shootings occur.

Who is to blame, then? The person using a gun to harm innocent people has the largest share of the blame, unless there are mitigating circumstances (e.g., age, mental illness). Politicians share some of the blame as well. They realize the scope of the problem but fail to take action or craft laws that could reduce gun violence. The gun industry is morally liable as well. Irresponsible gun owners are partially to blame. Apathetic and uninformed voters are also part of the problem. Because the NRA, through its influence, has contributed to the proliferation of guns and easier access to them, it must also shoulder some of the blame.

4. "They Want to Take Our Guns Away from Us!"

Many gun owners were worried that Barack Obama was planning to "take their guns away" during his presidency. Donald Trump stoked these fears: "You know, the President is thinking about signing an executive order where he wants to take your guns away. You hear about this? Not gonna happen. That won't happen. But that's a tough one, I think that's a tough one for him to do."[14] Of course, this never happened. Obama's second term ended. People still had their guns.

Many people worry that "the elites" want to take their guns away. At the 2018 Conservative Political Action Conference, just days after the high school shooting in Parkland, Florida, head of the NRA Wayne LaPierre said, "The elites don't care not one whit about America's school system and school children. If they truly cared, what they would do is they would protect them. For them it's not a safety issue, it's a political issue. They care more about control and more of it, their goal is to eliminate the Second Amendment and our firearms freedoms so that they can eradicate all individual freedoms."[15] It's not just guns that they want to take away, but all our individual liberties. This rhetoric is effective, but it is false. LaPierre gives no evidence for these claims, and they are without merit.

Many worry that if additional restrictions are placed upon buying and owning firearms, it will be very difficult and perhaps impossible for responsible people to do so. In a *New York Times*/CBS News poll, 52 percent believed that it was at least somewhat likely that "stricter gun laws will eventually lead to the federal government trying to take away guns from Americans who legally own them."[16] Is this a valid concern? No. The argument that adding more restrictive gun laws will lead to a ban on gun ownership commits the slippery slope fallacy. This fallacy occurs when someone claims that an apparently harmless action will lead to a terrible outcome. For example,

> Bans on so-called assault weapons must be vigorously opposed. Once the gun-grabbing liberals have outlawed assault weapons, next they'll go after handguns. After that, it will be shotguns and semiautomatic hunting rifles. In the end, law-abiding citizens will be left totally defenseless against predatory criminals and a tyrannical government.[17]

Not all arguments commit this fallacy. If there are good reasons for thinking that the bad outcome will result from what appears to be a harmless act, then this can be a sound form of argument. This leaves us with an important question. Are there good reasons for thinking that the addition of more restrictive gun laws will lead to a complete ban on all firearms, leaving "law-abiding citizens . . . totally defenseless against predatory criminals and a tyrannical government"? For many, the answer is obviously yes, while others believe it is clearly no. Who is right? It's difficult to see how the Second Amendment would be repealed in the United States. Given the decisions made by the Supreme Court, especially in the 2008 *Heller* case, there are significant barriers in place. Is it impossible? No. Is it highly unlikely? Yes. The current restrictions on firearms have not produced an all-out ban. The laws in place restricting ownership of fully automatic weapons are one example. And the now-defunct federal law banning assault weapons did not lead to further bans on handguns, shotguns, or hunting rifles. In fact, Congress let the ban die out back in 2004.

Nevertheless, some believe that the Second Amendment should be repealed. In March of 2018, former Supreme Court justice John Paul Stevens published an op-ed in the *New York Times* calling for this very thing.[18] Stevens, one of the four dissenters in the *Heller* case, believes that the changes wrought by that decision would be reversed by this "simple but dramatic action." He maintains that the proper interpretation of the Second Amendment does not extend to an *individual* right to own a firearm, but rather indicates a right that has a "reasonable relation to the preservation or efficiency of a 'well regulated militia.'" Repealing this amendment "would make our schoolchildren safer than they have been since 2008 and honor the memories of the many, indeed far too many, victims of recent gun violence."

The changes I advocate later in this book do not call for such a repeal, and would not inexorably lead to the slippery slope feared by LaPierre and others. The changes I favor would retain sufficient protection for the rights contained in the Second Amendment. They would also put additional restrictions in place that would make all of us safer. No law or set of laws is perfect, however. In the next section, we will consider what this fact means for the gun debate.

5. "No Law Can Stop All Gun Violence"

Defenders of the status quo in America argue that no law can stop all gun violence, including mass shootings. They argue that people who want to get a gun in order to kill other people will find a way. They are criminals, after all. As Mike Huckabee puts the point, "Anyone who thinks we can simply ban guns and—poof—make them all disappear, even from the hands of criminals, is deluded."[19] Huckabee's way of putting things commits the straw-man fallacy. This fallacy occurs when someone misrepresents a position he or she disagrees with, in a way that makes it easier to criticize. For example:

> Mike claims that the Chiefs are a better team than the Steelers. But Joe says that the Steelers are not a bad team. They have a good quarterback, great receivers, and a strong defense. Joe concludes that Mike does not know what he's talking about here.

Joe has committed the straw-man fallacy. Mike did not argue that the Steelers are a *bad* team, only that they are not *as good as* the Chiefs. Joe's description of Mike's argument distorted it. When people argue in this way, they do not provide proper support for their conclusions.

Huckabee has committed the straw-man fallacy. Granted, he's employing some rhetorical flourish here. But even so, this type of thing is persuasive to many. I'm not aware of anyone who has seriously argued that a gun ban would make all guns disappear or have a 100 percent success rate in keeping them out of the hands of criminals. The best arguments for more restrictive gun laws recognize that no law is foolproof. These arguments emphasize, however, that such laws *can reduce the likelihood* that some criminals will have access to guns, in turn reducing the overall level of gun violence. This is the heart of the issue—given that we cannot *eliminate* all gun violence, what can be done to *reduce* it? What can be done to make it *more difficult* for criminals to gain access to firearms?

Others who argue that no law can stop all gun violence avoid the straw-man fallacy but commit another mistake in reasoning, called the *all-or-nothing fallacy*.[20] David Kyle Johnson points out that after a mass shooting, when we engage in more intense debate of the issues, people argue that gun laws are useless. Criminals are, after all, criminals. They don't obey the law. Even with stricter laws, they will be able to get guns. But those laws will make it more difficult for law-abiding people to do so.

If a requirement for a valid law is 100 percent effectiveness, we'd have very few laws. If such effectiveness is necessary, we shouldn't have laws against murder, slavery, theft, assault, rape, and many more criminal acts, since those laws do not prevent *all* occurrences of these acts. But obviously we need such laws, because they deter some people from committing these crimes and they're required by justice.

Johnson points out another problem with such reasoning: laws are not usually a matter of all or nothing. The fact that many people continue to break the law by speeding does not mean there should be no speed limits. Laws are often crafted with the knowledge that they will not be 100 percent effective. Instead, the goal is to lower the frequency of the illegal behavior. This is true of laws against speeding, laws prohibiting the use of illegal drugs, and numerous other laws that are on the books. No law or set of laws will perfectly prevent criminals from getting and using guns. But this in no way means there should be no gun laws, or that stricter gun laws would be ineffective. The fact that some criminals will still find a way to get a gun in no way justifies inaction with respect to our current gun laws. If we make it more difficult for criminals to acquire guns, then fewer criminals will be able to do so. This is the middle ground that defenders of the status quo ignore when they commit the all-or-nothing fallacy.

6. "If Guns Are Outlawed, Then Only Outlaws Will Have Guns"

This claim has been around for decades. It can be seen on bumper stickers, banners, and across various social media. But what does it mean? What is its relevance for the gun debate? Is it true?

Like any if-then statement, this claim by itself is not an argument. Yet many people use it as one. We can craft the argument that the statement might communicate, on a literal interpretation:

> The result of outlawing guns is that only criminals would have guns.
> We should not create a situation in which only criminals have guns.
> *Therefore,*
> We should not outlaw guns.

For this argument to work, the first two claims must be true, and they must support the conclusion. The argument's first claim is clearly false. Even if all guns were made illegal, that is, if Congress repealed the Second Amendment, many law-abiding individuals would still possess and use firearms in the United States. Police officers and members of the armed forces jump to mind, as well as those who serve in the FBI, CIA, and Secret Service, among others. If guns are outlawed, then many who are not outlaws will still have guns. While most do not intend the argument to be taken so literally, part of what props it up is the fear that we will all be at the mercy of criminals if stricter gun laws are implemented. The argument plays on the fear of chaos. But even if the Second Amendment were abolished, it is false that only outlaws would have guns. I am not for abolishing the Second Amendment. But it is important to see the flaw in this argument.

Another, more charitable and plausible way to interpret the claim is that if guns were outlawed, then law-abiding people would be more vulnerable to harm by criminals. Criminals would have guns, but the rest of us would not. We would be at greater risk of becoming victims with no effective way of protecting ourselves. We would, literally, be outgunned. The argument can be put as follows:

> The result of outlawing guns is that law-abiding citizens could not defend themselves against criminals with guns.
> We should not create a situation in which law-abiding citizens could not defend themselves against criminals with guns.
> *Therefore,*
> We should not outlaw guns.

Some argue that this is the job of law enforcement. We should let trained professionals protect us from criminals with guns. However, in many cases the response time is not short enough for a person to depend on law enforcement for protection. The proposals I offer at the end of this book do not endorse abolishing gun rights. Rather, the aim is to make gun laws less liberal so that those who should not have guns will have a more difficult time getting them. Given this, law enforcement and responsible law-abiding individuals could still possess guns.

There is another way to interpret the statement. Perhaps what some mean by this claim is that if we outlaw guns, then many competent and law-abiding gun owners would refuse to forfeit their guns. Such people would now be criminals, because they would be disobeying gun laws. But these are good people who should not be forced to break laws prohibiting them from owning firearms.

7. "It's Not a Gun Problem, It's a Heart Problem"

As we should expect with clichés on matters of substance, this argument is not fully stated. The idea is that even if we restrict access to guns, people will still kill other people. If a person wants to kill someone, the person will find a way. Along these lines, many Christians like to point out that Cain killed Abel with a rock. This is meant to show that there is a problem with the human heart, namely, that we are prone to sin. Given this, even if we outlaw guns, people will still kill people. If we outlaw guns, people will use knives. If we outlaw knives, people will use rocks. Should we outlaw not only guns but also knives, rocks, cars, baseball bats, and everything else that people use to kill each other? To do so would be absurd. In *God, Guns, Grits, and Gravy*, Mike Huckabee expresses this thought as follows:

> Yes, guns can be dangerous. And in the wrong hands, the hands of someone who has a nefarious purpose or is careless and fails to respect the power of the firearm, or is mentally ill, they are dangerous. Fire in the hands of a cook is useful; fire in the hands

of a pyromaniac is deadly. Water can be for bathing or drowning. A pair of scissors can be for opening a box or stabbing someone. An airplane can be an incredibly efficient vehicle to travel between distances, or it can be a missile to be flown into buildings. I don't, however, hear any suggestions that we ban fire, water, scissors, or airplanes.[21]

The argument, then, is that the reason people use guns to kill others is that we are fundamentally flawed. Those who state that "Guns don't kill people, people kill people" likely have this in mind. The issue is not guns. It is us. We can't legislate morality into the human heart. More restrictive gun laws will not transform the hearts of those who would seek to hurt or kill others. Rather than creating more laws, we should focus on helping people deal with their heart/sin problem.

This argument is appealing because it contains some important truths. We do have a heart problem. We are morally and spiritually flawed beings. Human nature is fallen and weak. A change in gun laws will not in and of itself change human nature. Even if we could effectively restrict or abolish access to guns, murders would still happen. People would use knives, or follow the lead of Cain and use a rock.

However, there are problems with this argument.

First, the argument poses a false dilemma. This fallacy occurs when someone presents a false either/or choice in an argument. Here the assumption is, since we have a heart problem, guns aren't the real issue. Therefore, we do not need to craft more restrictive gun laws. But why believe this? Why believe that it is *either* a heart *or* a gun problem? Surely it is possible that we have *both* a heart problem *and* a gun problem. It seems clear that we do have both problems. In fact, we already recognize this. The National Firearms Act of 1934 (and its modifications in 1968 and 1986) contains strict regulations governing fully automatic weapons. Under federal law, citizens cannot own a fully automatic weapon that was manufactured after May 19, 1986. They can own such weapons manufactured prior to this, but the process for obtaining one is fairly demanding. Given human nature, it should be. The laws that regulate private ownership of fully automatic firearms are based in part on the fact that human beings are morally flawed. We flawed creatures should not possess the power to efficiently kill or maim large numbers of people.

The problem, then, is both easy access to guns and the human heart. While guns don't kill people, people often use guns to kill people. And guns make it easier to do so, given the capacity a gun has to harm others in a relatively quick and efficient manner. Whatever solutions we adopt should address the problems posed by the human heart and by easy access to guns.

A second problem with the argument is that the comparison between guns and other methods of killing is flawed. Many guns are specifically designed to kill large numbers of human beings in a short period of time, with relative ease. This is not the case for knives, cars, baseball bats, or rocks. On the same day as the mass shooting in Newtown, Connecticut, a man attacked and stabbed twenty-two children and one adult at a primary school in China. While this shows that laws will not prevent all violent crime, it does highlight an important difference between guns and knives. All the victims of the knife attack in China survived. Twenty-six people died at Sandy Hook Elementary. There are cases in which large numbers of people have been killed by a person wielding a knife.[22] In 2016, a former employee carried out an attack at a residential facility in Japan for persons with disabilities. He entered the facility at 2:00 a.m. and killed nineteen people and injured another twenty-six with a knife. Weapons other than guns can be used to carry out mass killings. However, it is more difficult and more rare. Guns tend to be more efficient and more lethal.

Cars also have the potential to kill large numbers of people in a short period of time. But again, they are not designed for that purpose. Numerous regulations are in place to reduce the risk of this happening, intentionally or accidentally, because of the potential for harm. And we have many laws in place to prevent people from turning airplanes into missiles. The same reasoning applies to guns. More restrictive and effective laws should be in place to reduce the risk of people using guns to harm others.

Third, the fact that humans have a sin problem actually supports the argument for more rational and restrictive gun laws. Given our fallen nature, surely we should not allow easy access to weapons that make it easy to kill lots of people quickly. If laws are not relevant to changing human hearts, or at least to restricting the human ability to do evil, then why do some support laws restricting abortion? Why do others support laws concerning prejudice based on race or gender? After all, even with such laws in place, abortions will still occur and prejudice remains alive and well. One reason is that the law can function to deter us from making some choices, even if our hearts remain unchanged. Laws can protect others from the harm we might do apart from their restraining power. The same justifications exist for guns. Of course, gun laws cannot unilaterally change the human heart. But they can make it more difficult for that fallen heart to express its evil intentions through the barrel of a gun.

Stricter gun laws are not a panacea. We must not think that simply changing the laws will solve the problem of gun violence in America. We also need to address the many other issues that are present. We have a culture of violence and death, a waning respect for the dignity of all human beings, and a host of other problems and needs that must be addressed. For Christians, the central way to do this is with the gospel of Jesus Christ. We can exemplify and invite others into life with God. But this must not be done in lieu of crafting and enforcing more effective laws. Rather, we must do both as we seek to bring the reality of God's kingdom to bear in our world.

8. "The Only Thing That Stops a Bad Person with a Gun Is a Good Person with a Gun"

In the wake of the mass church shooting in Sutherland Springs, Texas, many were calling for arming people in church. In response to a claim in *Newsweek* that the good-guy-with-a-gun theory had been deeply discredited, an editor for the *Federalist* wrote, "Though an incontrovertible truth for many media, it's not really a 'theory,' much less deeply discredited. It is a fact that the only real way to stop a 'bad guy' with a gun is a 'good guy' with a gun, whether that person be in law enforcement or a private citizen."[23] As we'll see, it is not a fact. It is quite clearly false that "the only real way" to stop a bad guy with a gun is a good guy with a gun.

This same mind-set, however, is espoused by NRA executive Wayne LaPierre. He maintains that if we want to stop mass shootings and other gun crimes, we don't need more restrictive gun laws. Rather, the only thing that will successfully stop a bad guy with a gun is a good guy with a gun. There are certainly cases in which bad guys with guns have been stopped by good people with guns.[24] In many of these cases, police officers are able to stop the offenders. But LaPierre's point is that regular citizens should be armed in order to stop bad guys with guns. Several cases in which bad guys with guns were stopped by good guys with guns were noted earlier in the chapter, as was the statistic that firearms are used approximately 58,500 times per year in self-protection against attempted or actual violent crime.[25]

But the claim that the *only* thing that can stop a bad guy with a gun is a good guy with a gun is clearly and demonstrably false. It can be refuted by numerous counterexamples.

First, consider a case in which a bad guy with a gun was stopped by a good woman with a Bible, a Christian book, and the virtues of faith, hope, and love. On March 11, 2005, Brian Nichols was being taken to court in Atlanta on charges of rape. He was able to get a court deputy's gun and then shoot and kill the judge, a court reporter, and another deputy as he fled. He also killed a federal agent. Nichols took refuge in the apartment of Ashley Smith, holding her at gunpoint. She recognized him as the subject of the manhunt and cooperated with him. They began to talk about God and family, and she shared from a passage in Rick Warren's book *The Purpose-Driven Life*, describing the value of serving God and others. Eventually Nichols agreed to let Smith leave to pick up her daughter. From her car Smith called 911, and police surrounded the apartment. Nichols surrendered. Smith believes that during their conversation, Nichols began to want to follow God's will for his life, which ultimately led him to release her.[26]

On April 22, 2015, early morning shots rang out in a Nashville, Tennessee, Waffle House. James Shaw Jr. immediately ran into the restroom and hid from the gunman. But he didn't stay there. Shaw watched the gunman, and when he paused to look at his rifle, Shaw sprang into action. Unarmed, he rushed the gunman and disarmed him. In the confrontation, his arm was grazed by a bullet, but he was able to wrestle the gun away and throw it behind the counter, which caused the gunman to flee. Four people were murdered that day, but many more would likely have died if Shaw had not acted in such a heroic manner. As one witness put it, "He was a hero. . . . Had that guy had a chance to reload his weapon, there was plenty more people in that restaurant."[27]

Consider other counterexamples to LaPierre's claim. There are different techniques one can use (that do not involve a gun) to disarm an assailant who is armed with a gun. Or one might carry and use a taser gun as a means of self-defense. My point is not that we should solely depend on these methods. I believe responsible and competent individuals have the right to own and use a gun for self-defense. Nevertheless, the foregoing shows that the belief that only a good guy with a gun can stop a bad buy with a gun is false.

And not only that, but the alleged good guys with guns often turn out to be either criminals or careless. Concealed-carry permit holders, seemingly prime candidates for being the good guy with a gun, were in fact responsible for killing 1,129 people in the United States since 2007.[28] This includes homicides, suicides, and unintentional deaths. It does not include cases that are legally determined to be instances of self-defense. This figure includes twenty-one law enforcement officers, killed by holders of such permits. This does not justify eliminating such permits. But it does give good reason for thinking about the process of obtaining concealed-carry permits, and whether it should be more rigorous.

Often lost in this debate are accidental shootings of innocent people, including cases in which such individuals are mistaken for intruders or threats. Consider a twenty-one-year-old woman who hid in a closet with her younger sister, to surprise her fiancé. When they jumped out of the closet, he used a .40 caliber Glock, which he kept for self-defense, to kill her. In another case, a young mother heard noises on the gravel outside her home. There had been recent reports of a burglary, so she retrieved a handgun from her bedroom.

She accidentally shot and killed her infant son while looking out the window for an intruder. And in a third instance, a fourteen-year-old girl was hiding in her closet when her parents returned home in the middle of the night. She jumped out and yelled, "Boo." Her father thought she was an intruder. He shot and killed her. The last thing she said was "I love you, Daddy."[29]

Even good people make mistakes. Sometimes, those mistakes are fatal.

Moreover, we have a theological reason to be skeptical of the good-person-with-a-gun claim. Its view of human nature is too optimistic. At times, the presence of a gun can exacerbate our flaws. Consider the highly publicized case of George Zimmerman, who was put on trial for shooting and killing teenager Trayvon Martin. John Donohue, professor of law at Stanford University and coauthor of a National Bureau of Economic Research study on gun violence and concealed-carry laws, is skeptical of the good-guy-with-a-gun claim in this and other cases. He says possessing a gun likely encouraged Zimmerman to confront Martin. In many cases, the "good guys" are encouraged to be more aggressive because they are armed. The result is that people die who otherwise would not. According to Donohue, "It's not very often that somebody with a gun who's a private citizen plays a useful role in ending . . . mass shooting events."[30] On a Christian view of human nature, all human beings are fallen. Even the best of us are flawed. As followers of Jesus, we must take this into account as we consider these issues.

Lack of training can also undermine good guys with guns from effectively using those guns. Former Bureau of Alcohol, Tobacco, and Firearms agent David Chipman contends that armed civilians often lack the training needed to effectively use a gun when bullets are coming at them. He believes that the good-guy-with-a-gun slogan is more about encouraging gun sales, based on an unrealistic optimism people have concerning their ability to win a gun battle.[31]

I would add that there is also an unrealistic optimism concerning their ability to pick out the bad guy and only the bad guy. This is true even for trained police officers, as a tragedy in Alabama shows. On Thanksgiving night 2018, E. J. Bradford was shot by an off-duty police officer working security at an Alabama shopping mall. Two people were shot at the mall, and police initially identified Bradford as the shooter. They were wrong. Bradford had his own gun out and was trying to offer help at the scene when he was shot in the back because he was mistakenly thought to be the gunman. The actual gunman was later arrested. An additional problem is underscored by this case. As a lawyer for the Bradford family put it, if you're black, then it "does not matter if you are a good guy with a gun."[32]

In *Costly Grace*, Rob Schenck expresses these concerns well in a discussion with three of his friends. As they argue back and forth, one of Schenck's friends tells him that if he's afraid of guns, he should just let others have and use them, stating, "I'm not afraid of guns." In reply Schenck says, "You know one of the reasons that I'm afraid of them? Because I don't trust *myself* in the moment of crisis when I'm awash in adrenaline. I do not trust *my* judgment, and I'm amazed at how much you trust yours. I'm amazed by that."[33] This healthy mistrust of oneself is wise, and it serves to undermine the good-guy-with-a-gun claim.

Consider some relevant data related to guns, self-defense, and deterrence in the United States. Some argue that the number of times a gun is used in self-defense is much greater than the 58,500 referenced above, citing a 1995 study that claimed there are 2.5 million cases of Americans using guns for self-defense each year.[34] This claim, however, is simply not plausible.[35] When one examines the statistics in more detail, the absurd conclusions that result reveal why. In this study, 34 percent of respondents said their use of a gun in self-defense occurred during a burglary. This would mean that guns were used in self-defense in about 845,000 burglaries. But victimization surveys indicate fewer than 6 million burglaries in the year of this survey, only 1.3 million of which involved victims who were at home at the time of the burglary. Two-thirds of those victims were asleep. If we also factor in the fact that 41 percent of US households include gun owners, we reach the absurd conclusion, based on the 2.5 million number, that victims of burglaries used guns in self-defense *over* 100 percent of the time. More reliable studies conclude that the total is somewhere between 55,000 and 120,000 per year.

Why does this matter? First, it matters because truth matters. Second, reasonable gun policies should be based on sound data, so that we can craft and enforce appropriate and effective policies. Third, the larger numbers incite and exacerbate the fear that many people have, a fear that often motivates their positions and actions related to these issues. This is true on all sides, but it must be noted here. Christians, of course, have a very good reason to avoid acquiring beliefs or making decisions based on fear. Our decisions should ultimately be grounded in our faith in God and the security we experience by being recipients of his love under his providential care.

LaPierre and others who make this claim about the unique ability of good guys with guns seem to assume that it is impossible to prevent bad guys from obtaining guns in the first place. But this commits the fallacy of begging the question, insofar as it assumes something that is at issue in the gun debates. Proponents of more restrictive gun laws argue that they can keep many bad guys from obtaining guns in the first place. The claim that our only defense here is a good guy with a gun must be argued for, and not merely assumed or asserted. But there are more restrictive gun laws that would allow responsible persons to own and use guns for self-defense. As David Hemenway points out, "Reasonable gun policies—such as requiring manufacturers to meet minimum safety standards or requiring background checks on sales at gun shows—would have little effect on the ability of responsible adults in the United States to defend themselves with guns."[36]

9. "Guns Make Us Free"

Gun-rights advocates claim that our Second Amendment rights ensure that all our other rights are protected. LaPierre and the NRA contend that the Second Amendment "is the one freedom that gives common men and women uncommon power to defend all freedoms."[37] Gun rights protect all our other rights. If we undermine them, we're undermining freedom.

Many gun-rights advocates believe that freedom involves being alert to the potential threats around us in our daily lives. We must always be on guard, ready to defend ourselves with a gun. But is this genuine freedom? Genuine freedom is something else. It "is the resolve to coexist with pervasive threats and not be overly influenced or coerced by them. Freedom is a state of mental resolve, not armed resolve. . . . It's no sign of freedom to live always at the ready, worried and trigger-happy, against potential threats; this is the opposite of freedom" (45).

Guns undermine the freedom from fear in everyday life, from concern over potential threats, that we should all desire. But what about our political freedoms? Do we need guns to protect them in the way the NRA and many gun-rights advocates claim? Do guns "carve out the necessary space for us to act and exist as free, democratic citizens" (143)?

The answer, again, is no. The ubiquitous presence of guns can signify a lack of freedom, because it signifies a lack of security. If I cannot feel safe walking down the street, going to church, going to a movie, or going out to eat without a gun on my person, how free am I? If the rule of law is this powerless, then society looks more like the war of all against all than it does a civil, democratic, or law-governed society.

Guns are not a sign of freedom or security. They are often a sign of fear and insecurity. There are cases, of course, where guns save lives. But "they bring no enduring safety. At best, they maintain a tense, fragile substitute, like the electric détente when two warring gangs hold each other off with pointed weapons. . . . In our American democracy, we have higher ambitions" (157–58).

Democracy flourishes when there are open dialogue and debate, and the freedom to engage in peaceful protest without being intimidated by the threat of force. Guns are in many ways incompatible with two rights that are essential to a healthy democracy: the right to free speech and the right to assembly. When there is violence, or the threat of it, including when people openly carry guns in the public square, free speech is chastened and assembly is discouraged. In 2009, guns were present at protests against the Affordable Care Act (176–77). People showed up at appearances by

President Obama with their guns. One man in Phoenix had an AR-15 and a handgun in a holster on his hip, arguing with people who supported the act. In New Hampshire, a man with a holstered gun carried a sign that read "It is time to water the tree of liberty." This is a reference to Thomas Jefferson's claim that "The tree of liberty must be refreshed from time to time with the blood of patriots and tyrants." This man seemed to be stating that violence was called for to stop Obama (and maybe his supporters) from passing the act. As one political scientist observed, "When you start to bring guns to political rallies, it does layer on another level of concern and significance. It actually becomes quite scary for many people. It creates a chilling effect in the ability of our society to carry on honest communication" (178).

This is exactly right. Guns don't protect freedom of speech. They silence it. Our freedom, our equality, should be protected by the rule of law. If our rights must be secured, day in and day out, by force or the threat of it, then we have departed from the vision of our founding fathers. They sought a society governed by the rule of law, not one where we must depend on force to secure our rights. It is "the protection of laws" that we need, as this "is the great relief that civil society offers" (188).

The commitment of some in the gun-rights movement to democratic institutions can be called into question in other ways. Sharron Angle, a 2010 Republican candidate for a Nevada Senate seat, warned that if Republicans didn't gain a majority in Congress, if they didn't win at the ballot box, then people would be "afraid that they'll have to fight for their liberty in Second Amendment kinds of ways" (190–91). In March 2012, a column in a Republican newsletter in Virginia called for an armed revolution if Obama won reelection. The only recourse left, if they failed to defeat Obama, was armed revolution, because our "Republic cannot survive for 4 more years underneath this political socialist ideologue."[38]

Threatening to use force when one cannot win at the ballot box is antithetical to democracy. These attitudes and the actions they produce are the true threats to democracy and freedom, not the laws that would merely seek to make it more difficult for criminals and persons who are a danger to others or themselves to acquire a gun. Unfortunately, and ironically, many gun-rights advocates cannot see this truth.

10. "Guns Protect Us from Tyranny and Genocide"

Many advocates of the status quo regarding gun laws in the United States claim that guns protect citizens from a potentially tyrannical government. An armed populace serves to deter the government from infringing on our rights. For example, Mike Huckabee claims that "the purpose of the Second Amendment was . . . to make sure we can protect our freedoms from those who would take them away—including our own government, should it become as tyrannical as the one that launched the revolution in the first place."[39]

We saw in chapter 1 that the purpose of the Second Amendment may not be as clear as Huckabee makes it out to be. Nevertheless, in 2008 a majority of Supreme Court justices agreed that an armed citizens' militia serves as a "safeguard against tyranny." Many Americans contend that the right to own a gun is justified in part by the belief that guns are a bulwark against tyranny. Surveys show that many people in the United States associate the private ownership of firearms with values like liberty, individualism, self-reliance, and distrust of the government.[40] In light of this, many contend that any additional restrictions related to firearms is tantamount to an assault on our liberty and the rights granted to us by God.

Let's consider the logic of the view that guns serve this function—a bulwark against tyranny—in contemporary America. In 2018, Kirsten Powers and Jonathan Merritt discussed this on their podcast *The Faith Angle*.[41] In response to those who hold that the purpose of the right to own firearms is to prevent tyranny, Merritt points out that nowadays the government can kill whomever it likes, without entering your home. One sufficiently armed drone is enough to end the lives of purported enemies of the state. Powers does not rule out the possibility that the US government could become totalitarian. She agrees with Merritt that it would be hard to fight off the United States military, even if the populace was well armed with a variety of firearms. If such a situation were ever to come about, she believes it is likely that the military would be a stabilizing force. I think she is right about this, and about the larger point that totalitarianism could happen here. Military men and women swear an oath to uphold the Constitution, not a particular political leader or group of leaders. But of course, there is no guarantee that the power of the military will never be used on American citizens under the orders of a tyrannical government.

The discussion on *The Faith Angle* raises some important points. If one justification for the right to bear arms is defense against tyranny, how far does that justification go? Given the might of the military and the advanced and highly destructive weapons of war it possesses, it could be argued that the citizens' militia needs more than handguns and semiautomatic weapons. It also needs fully automatic weapons, rocket-propelled grenades, surface-to-air missiles, tanks, properly equipped aircraft, and even weapons of mass destruction in order to deter potential tyranny or to overthrow a tyrannical government. Andrew Napolitano, former New Jersey Superior Court judge and current Fox News analyst, appears to agree with this. He argues that "The historical reality of the Second Amendment's protection of the right to keep and bear arms is not that it protects the right to shoot deer. It protects the right to shoot tyrants, and it protects the right to shoot at them effectively, thus, with the same instruments they would use upon us."[42]

But this last part is simply absurd. It is beyond the pale of reason and common sense to argue that individuals should have "the same instruments" that some hypothetical future tyrannical government would possess. Do we really want a world in which individual civilians have access to tanks, surface-to-air missiles, military aircraft, or weapons of mass destruction?

It is not just common sense and reason that reject this sort of nonsense. The *Heller* decision recognizes that the types of weapons one can own can be justifiably limited (e.g., machine guns), certain people can be prohibited from owning them (felons, people with certain mental illnesses), and there are certain places where they cannot be carried (in schools, government buildings). If such weapons were widely available, the chances that they would be employed for some nefarious purpose are much greater than the chances that they would be needed for a defense against tyranny.

At times, advocates of the view that guns are a bulwark against tyranny also claim that an unarmed citizenry is susceptible to genocide, pointing to Hitler's Nazi Germany as an example of this. Huckabee argues that one reason the Nazis were able to commit genocide against the Jews is that they had guns and the Jews did not. The Nazis removed guns from Jewish homes and outlawed possession of guns by Jews. They knew who had guns, according to Huckabee, because prior to Hitler's rise to power, a law was passed in 1928 requiring the police to keep records concerning gun ownership. And in early 1938, Hitler passed more gun-control laws. Furthermore, Huckabee reports that the staunchest resistance faced by the Nazis was in the 1943 Warsaw ghetto uprising. The Polish resisters were outnumbered and outgunned, but they were able to put up a fight before being overcome because they had some handguns.[43]

Huckabee's characterization is incorrect in some important ways.[44] As Philip Cook and Kristin Goss point out, in the large volume of works written by historians about the Nazis, little to no attention has been given to the possible role that gun laws played in all that occurred during this terrible period. Moreover, the first to offer up the argument that strict gun-control laws fostered Nazi genocide were American lawyers and activists opposed to more restrictive gun laws. Of course, this does not mean they are wrong. That would be fallacious reasoning. As Cook and Goss point out, the fact that historians have paid little attention to the role of gun laws in the Nazi rise to power "is either a terrible oversight or a telling omission."[45]

It is the case, however, that prior to Hitler's rise to power in 1933, gun laws in Germany were becoming more permissive. After World War I, guns were banned in Germany and people were ordered to surrender them, as well as any ammunition they had. Then, in 1928, things began to change. A system of licensing was implemented governing both the manufacture and sale of firearms. Some people were now allowed to own, carry, make, and transfer possession of firearms. In 1938, Hitler actually relaxed the laws even further, removing the licensing requirement for shotguns and rifles and lowering the age of legal gun ownership to eighteen. According to this law, however, Jews in Germany were not allowed to manufacture guns or ammunition, and soon after they were no longer allowed to possess either. They were also ordered to surrender their weapons or face twenty years in a concentration camp. Subsequent to these events, the Nazi genocide began.

Gun-rights advocates conclude from this that when gun laws are restrictive, and owners of firearms have to register their weapons with the government, the people are more vulnerable to tyranny and genocide. Those on the other side counter that it is ludicrous to contend that the small and despised Jewish people would have been a match for the Nazi military and police forces without a substantial number of gentiles taking up arms to fight alongside them. No direct evidence of the use of a gun registry to raid particular Jewish homes has ever been presented. In fact, prior to gun-control laws being enacted against the Jewish people, Hitler had engaged in a widespread assault on other important rights and liberties. Freedom of speech and freedom of association were suspended. The government's search and seizure powers were broadened. The homes of Jews and other political enemies were ransacked. Parliament was dissolved. In this situation, a right to bear arms would have been just one of many other rights suppressed by the state.

This issue is not merely of interest to "the lunatic fringe," as Daniel Polsby and Don Kates put it, in their study of the connection between a society's gun-control laws and the likelihood of genocide occurring in that society.[46] They admit that there are many steps between being disarmed and becoming a victim of genocide. But they also point out that in the dozens of principal genocides that occurred in the twentieth century, every population victimized was unarmed. "An armed population is simply more difficult to exterminate than one that is defenseless."[47] And they are surely right about this. They are also correct that an armed populace cannot necessarily defeat a government carrying out a genocide, but it can increase the costs that would be incurred. This could deter a government considering such actions. In addition, many who oppose stricter gun laws are concerned that even under the Constitution, our government could "degenerate into the sort of pitiless totalitarian instrument that has, at one time or another, afflicted most of the peoples of the Old and Third Worlds."[48] They point to the fact that genocide and tyranny have occurred, even in advanced civilizations.

However, if a tyrannical or despotic government wanted to carry out genocide in the United States today, it would have many more effective ways to go about it than were available in 1943 (or even in 1997). With this in mind, in the end an armed population would likely be at the mercy of that government. Even granting the points raised by Polsby and Kates about unarmed populations and genocide, the level of military technology available to the US government today is far greater.

Why does this matter? If some future United States government became tyrannical, or even decided to carry out genocide, it is much more likely it would employ weapons of mass destruction, such as chemical or biological weapons, small nuclear weapons, or even conventional weapons launched from unmanned drones, than go house to house as the Nazis did in Warsaw. It is beyond the pale of all sound reason to think that civilians should have access to such weapons as a possible deterrent, given the much greater likelihood that these weapons would be misused and lead to the deaths of innocent people than used to mount a defense against some future genocidal or tyrannical American government.

From a Christian as well as a more general moral perspective, it seems both more reasonable and more practical to strengthen the structures and institutions within society that can prevent tyranny or genocide. The system of checks and balances our founders put in place is one important aspect of this, as is the rule of law. Surely preventing tyranny and genocide by such means is the better option. If so, our time is better spent making these structures and institutions as impervious as possible to those who would violate them for immoral ends.

Christian conservatives often express fear of tyranny, and distrust and even hatred of government, and the need to have an armed populace. But Wayne Grudem, a very politically and theologically conservative scholar, observes that government is seen as a good thing by Paul in Romans 13:1-7. Paul writes that the government "is God's servant for your good." Governments do fail to fulfill this purpose, but "we should view civil government as a gift from God. . . . *The institution of civil government* in itself is something very good, a benefit that flows to us from God's infinite wisdom and love."[49] Christians who are hostile toward the government as an institution should rethink this attitude. Not all governments are on the brink of becoming tyrannical.

In sum, how should we answer the question of whether there is a connection between more restrictive gun laws and the likelihood of tyranny or genocide? As Cook and Goss conclude, "The simplest and perhaps least satisfying answer is that we don't have enough data to judge."[50] To conclude that guns do preserve freedom in these ways, on the basis of good evidence, we would need to compare democracies that have an armed populace where freedom is preserved with democracies that are similar in all the relevant ways but with strict gun-control laws that became tyrannical. But there are not enough nations in either of these categories to justify any such conclusions. Even the claim that the case of the United States supports the view that guns or institutions are better safeguards lacks a rational basis. America is ambiguous here, because it has both strong democratic institutions and a well-armed population.

If the rule of law and strong democratic institutions can preserve liberty, individual rights, and the common good, we should do all we can to ensure that they do so. This is a more humane way to protect these goods. Even a well-armed population can do little against the military might of some future hypothetical tyrannical government.

Conclusion

In this chapter, we've been able to examine several falsehoods and fallacies that are often present in debates concerning guns, gun violence, morality, and the law. Most of the cliché-style arguments that are either false or fallacious are given by those who prefer that we maintain the status quo with respect to gun laws in the United States, and the content of this chapter reflects that reality. Other falsehoods and fallacies not covered in this chapter will emerge in the discussion that follows. There are also, to be sure, more substantive arguments present on all sides of this debate. In the coming chapters, we will examine these arguments from a Christian ethical perspective. The next chapter focuses on several key issues related to Christian thought on violence and how it relates to gun issues.

4

VIOLENCE, GUNS, AND THE GOSPEL

"How might members of the body of Christ think more faithfully about guns and gun violence in light of Christian peculiarity and the doctrine of the Kingdom of God?"

This poignant question was asked by Charles Marsh, a professor of religious studies at the University of Virginia, in his article "The NRA's Assault on Christian Faith and Practice."[1] Marsh asks many provocative and important questions. In the prophetic tradition, he challenges followers of Christ to consider this question in light of the alliance between the NRA and many white evangelicals in the United States.

Data from a 2017 Pew Research Center study reveals that white evangelicals are more likely than people of other faith groups to own a gun.[2] Forty-one percent of white evangelicals possess a firearm, compared to just 30 percent of all Americans. In recent years, some prominent Christian leaders have called for congregants or students at Christian universities to arm themselves. Pastor Robert Jeffress of First Baptist Church in Dallas proudly estimates that from 25 to 50 percent of his congregation is armed on any given Sunday.[3] After the San Bernardino shooting, Jerry Falwell Jr., president of Liberty University, announced that all students would be able to take a free concealed-carry class. He said, "If more good people had concealed-carry permits, then we could end those Muslims before they walked in and killed them." He encouraged Liberty students to "teach them a lesson if they ever show up here."[4]

As Marsh notes, all of this puts evangelical followers of Jesus in a strange place. Jesus tells Peter to put his sword away in the Garden of Gethsemane. He warns that those who live by the sword will die by the sword. Athanasius, a fourth-century defender of Christian orthodoxy, wrote that Christians, "instead of arming themselves with swords, extend their hands in prayer."[5] Christians don't have to be pacifists to observe a tension, if not a contradiction, between the views of these evangelicals and the teachings of Jesus about forgiveness, reconciliation, love, and "the preferential option for nonviolence."[6]

American Christians, especially evangelicals, need to look at the teachings of Jesus and ask themselves and others some very pointed questions about the relationship among faith, weapons, and violence. We need a robust theological discussion focused on violence, guns, and what can be done in the United States to deal with these issues. This kind of discussion is what I offer in the remaining pages of this book.

Pacifism, Justified Violence, and Peace Building

Broadly speaking, the two main views concerning violence in the Christian tradition are pacifism and defense of just war. The former, pacifism, is the view that violence is simply wrong. Christians should not participate in it. We should seek nonviolent solutions to our problems, whether personal or political. The latter, just war/justified violence, maintains that there are times when violence is regrettably necessary. The paradigm cases of this are self-defense and defense of other people.

There is a third view, which I call *peace building*. This view rejects the pacifist belief that violence is always wrong and absolutely prohibited. But, given the values intrinsic to the gospel—including the inherent value and dignity of all human life—peace building allows for violence *only as a last resort* and includes a very strong preference for nonviolence. Peace building is distinct from defense of or participation in just war in that it takes seriously the use of violence as a last resort, an idea endorsed but rarely followed by defenders of just war.

Supporters of just-war theory seem to justify the necessity of violence after the fact rather than as a check on the human impulse to violence. Peace building takes seriously the idea that violence may be justified in a particular situation but is not always necessary. A peace builder seeks and pursues peace; violence is only an act of last resort. This is important for the arguments of this book. My criticisms of many of the current Christian attitudes and perspectives in America concerning gun ownership and use do not depend on a commitment to pacifism (even though pacifism has much to commend it from a Christian point of view).

Pacifism

In his acceptance speech upon receiving the Nobel Peace Prize in 1964, Martin Luther King Jr. said:

> Nonviolence is the answer to the crucial political and moral question of our time—the need for man to overcome oppression and violence without resorting to violence and oppression. . . . Sooner or later all the people of the world will have to discover a way to live together in peace, and thereby transform this pending cosmic elegy into a creative psalm of brotherhood. If this is to be achieved, man must evolve for all human conflict a method which rejects revenge, aggression and retaliation. The foundation of such a method is love.[7]

King powerfully expresses the Christian pacifist position and its foundation of love.

As briefly noted above, pacifism is the view that engaging in acts of violence is never justified, either in war or in one's personal life. A pacifist will not participate in war, at least in the aspects of it that involve violent acts. Neither will a pacifist use violence in personal life, either in self-defense or in defense of others. But pacifism is not the same thing as passivity. King, for example, actively resisted violence and evil through nonviolent means. Our focus is on pacifism in the personal realm, and what it entails for the follower of Christ who embraces it.

Pacifists contend that violence is the way of the world, not the way of Christ, whose kingdom is not of this world. Numerous biblical texts support pacifism. For example, Christians do not wage war with the weapons of this world (2 Cor. 10:3-4). Our struggle is not against flesh and blood, and our weapons are spiritual in nature (Eph. 6:10-20). We are not to take vengeance on others, as Paul states in Romans 12:18-21. Rather, we are to "overcome evil with good." Jesus also blesses the peacemakers in Matthew 5.

One of the most central biblical texts used in support of pacifism comes from the Sermon on the Mount. Pacifists draw support from the following words of Jesus:

> "You have heard that it was said, 'An eye for an eye and a tooth for a tooth.' But I say to you, Do not resist an evildoer. But if anyone strikes you on the right cheek, turn the other also.... You have heard that it was said, 'You shall love your neighbor and hate your enemy.' But I say to you, Love your enemies and pray for those who persecute you, so that you may be children of your Father in heaven." (Matt. 5:38-39, 43-45)

For pacifists, these verses not only prevent participation in war but also apply to, for example, dealing with enemies in other contexts, including persecution, business, and in the church. Violence is not to be used, even in self-defense or in defense of others. Pacifists challenge the consistency of the claim that one can engage in acts of violence toward one's enemy and still love that enemy.

Pacifists also regularly appeal to the nonviolent response of Christ, as presented in 1 Peter 2:21, 23: "For to this you have been called, because Christ also suffered for you, leaving you an example, so that you should follow in his steps.... When he was abused, he did not return abuse; when he suffered, he did not threaten; but he entrusted himself to the one who judges justly." Pacifists argue that the very identity and mission of Christ include trusting God and not using violence to resist evil, even to the point of death on the cross. Pacifists call on Christians to entrust themselves to God and reject acts of violence, even to the point of death.

Pacifists understand Jesus's command to love one's enemies,

Paul's command to overcome evil with good, and the command in 1 Peter to imitate the nonviolence of Jesus as normative for his followers. Pacifists avoid violence as disciples of Jesus, the Prince of Peace. Pacifists seek peace.

Numerous biblical texts offer a compelling case for pacifism. Why, then, is pacifism not a more prominent view among Christians? Among many reasons, the simplest explanation is that many refuse to embrace the teachings of Jesus here.[8] Christians rationalize that (1) the words of Jesus are impractical, (2) the beatitudes and ethic of God's kingdom are for some future age, and (3) alternative solutions are needed in today's complex world. Sometimes this includes violence.

Despite these common objections, pacifists maintain that the reign of Jesus is not to be advanced by violence. Loving God entails that we love others, and this means that we forgo violence to reach our goals. It will be difficult. We may have to pay the ultimate price for our obedience to Christ. We are not called to pragmatism but rather to faithfulness. Discipleship has always involved a cross.[9]

Turning to pacifism as it relates to gun violence, Tim Suttle, a pastor in Kansas City, asks a pointed question, "Why do many Christians trust the Second Amendment more than the Sermon on the Mount?" His answer is troubling. Suttle claims that we simply don't believe that the way of Jesus will actually *work*.[10] I think there is something to this, but I also think there are principled reasons that apply.

Justified Violence

In contrast to pacifism, many Christians—past and present— argue for and participate in so-called just violence. Certain situations, it is claimed, require a violent response. Such justified violence is not only limited to nation-states (e.g., just war) but also pertains to violence between and among individuals.

Just-war theory rejects pacifism and holds that certain types of wars can be morally justified, a view that can be traced back to Augustine.[11] Prominent supporters of justified violence include

Thomas Aquinas, Francisco Suárez, and Hugo Grotius. Just-war theory makes several demands on supporters and participants. Some have to do with whether or not going to war is justified, while others focus on the moral requirements for carrying out war. Examining the entire theory isn't necessary, but looking at some aspects of it will be helpful.

The Bible and Justified Violence

Perhaps most important, Christian just-war theorists draw a distinction between killing and murder. Thus, on their reading, Exodus 20:13 prohibits murder but not all killing. Many just-war theorists also say Romans 13:1-7 provides support for their view:

> Let every person be subject to the governing authorities; for there is no authority except from God, and those authorities that exist have been instituted by God. Therefore whoever resists authority resists what God has appointed, and those who resist will incur judgment. For rulers are not a terror to good conduct, but to bad. Do you wish to have no fear of the authority? Then do what is good, and you will receive its approval; for it is God's servant for your good. But if you do what is wrong, you should be afraid, for the authority does not bear the sword in vain! It is the servant of God to execute wrath on the wrongdoer. Therefore one must be subject, not only because of wrath but also because of conscience. For the same reason you also pay taxes, for the authorities are God's servants, busy with this very thing. Pay to all what is due them—taxes to whom taxes are due, revenue to whom revenue is due, respect to whom respect is due, honor to whom honor is due.

The state's job is to enforce the law in order to maintain justice and social order. Thus, through the law and associated punishments, the state restrains evil. Further, this text is read to provide permission for individual Christians to use force in self-defense and the defense of others, as a member of law enforcement or the military.

The Bible is a violent book. There are passages detailing the conquest of Canaan, for example, that on a surface reading are troubling.[12] There are appeals to the book of Joshua, where the Israelites conquer their enemies with God's help. According to Joshua: "By this you shall know that among you is the living God who without fail will drive out from before you the Canaanites, Hittites, Hivites, Perizzites, Girgashites, Amorites, and Jebusites" (Josh. 3:10). But the Bible also warns against trusting in violence or weapons.[13] In Psalm 44:6 we read

> For not in my bow do I trust,
> nor can my sword save me.

In Proverbs, violence is usually associated with evil (Prov. 3:31; 13:2; 24:1–2). In the Old Testament, the reason God gives David for not allowing him to design and build the temple is: "You shall not build a house for my name, for you are a warrior and have shed blood" (1 Chron. 28:3).

Rules of Justified Violence

For a war to be just, it must be fought for a just cause. A war can be just if it is in self-defense against unprovoked aggression or done in defense of another nation that has suffered such aggression. A just war must also be fought with a right intention. This principle rules out wars of revenge, economic exploitation, or genocide. The intent must be a stable and fair peace for all parties. Crucially, a just war must be fought as a last resort. Other solutions, such as diplomatic talks or economic sanctions, must be exhausted before violence is decided upon.

Justified Violence and Guns

Just-war theory has some important implications for gun ownership and gun violence. By applying the principles of just-war theory to our individual lives, we can see how certain acts of violence may be morally justified. We'll refer to this as the justified violence view.

Just as nations have the right to defend themselves and other nations who are victims of aggression, so individuals have the right to self-defense and defense of others. If a person comes home and his spouse and children are being attacked by someone, and there is no time to wait on the police, then it is permissible and perhaps obligatory to stop the intruder, even if this involves killing him. If this is the only way to safeguard the family, then it is a morally just act. If this is correct, then we sometimes have a right to kill another person.

Some argue that this is one way to obey the law of loving your neighbor as yourself. How can the person in this hypothetical situation love his wife and children but not defend them? To refuse to act on their behalf seems like a refusal to love them. The problem is that this seems unloving to the intruder. But if he only intends to protect his family, while accepting (but not intending) the consequence that the intruder may be killed, then perhaps this problem is resolved.

The principle that a war must be fought only as a last resort is also applicable. If I am in a situation where my own life or the lives of others are potentially under threat, I have the moral responsibility to use force only as a last resort. Shooting first and asking questions later is unacceptable. There should be a strong presumption against the use of violence, including the use of a firearm.

Christian theorists use a variety of passages to support their view. In addition to Romans 13:1–7, Christians who justify violence point to Revelation 19:11 and Deuteronomy 20:10–20.[14]

Ironically, both pacifists and supporters of justified violence find ample support in Scripture. The Bible supports both positions. As such, its collective voice supports neither. There is another way: peace building.

Peace Building

We are too quick to turn to violence. Consider Dallas megachurch pastor Robert Jeffress, who, after the mass shooting at a Texas church, claimed that from 25 to 50 percent of his congregation have concealed-carry permits and that many bring their guns into church. "If somebody tries that in our church," he exclaimed, "they might get one shot off or two shots off, and that's the last thing they'll ever do in this life."[15] This is a nice line for a movie about the old American West, but coming from someone who is supposed to be a minister of the gospel, it is, from the perspective of peace building, simply unacceptable.

Scripture is replete with references to the value of peace and the obligation of followers of Jesus to foster peace in the world. In the Sermon on the Mount, Jesus blesses the peacemakers and commands his followers to love their enemies (Matt. 5:9, 44). In the letters of Paul, one of the fruits of the Holy Spirit is peace (Gal. 5:22-23), and it is clear from the context that this is not about inner personal peace, or at least not solely about it. It has to do with interpersonal relationships. The fruit of peace is contrasted with, among other things, "enmities, strife, jealousy, anger, quarrels, dissensions, factions" (Gal. 5:20). Psalm 34:14 encourages us to

> Depart from evil, and do good;
> seek peace, and pursue it.

Romans 14:17 tells us that "the kingdom of God is not food and drink but righteousness and peace and joy in the Holy Spirit." And finally, Romans 12:18 says, "If it is possible, so far as it depends on you, live peaceably with all."

Peace building, while allowing for situations in which violence is permissible, and even necessary, is distinct from the justified violence view. In this way it reflects the exhortation to live in peace with others, "so far as it depends on you." Peace building emphasizes the belief that violence should be used only as a last resort.

Peace builders do not claim that Christians should be left defenseless. Rather, they recognize that some passages of Scripture do seem to support the view that self-defense is permissible in some cases.[16] Exodus 22:2 allowed Israelites to kill an intruder who was breaking into their home at night. Other passages arguably give individuals and families a right to self-defense (see Neh. 4; Esther 8:11-14). Despite these texts, some would argue that the moral vision of Jesus given in the New Testament supersedes passages in the Old Testament that approve of violence, just as his teachings supersede passages about diet and circumcision.[17]

Regardless, the sentiments of some supporters of violence (e.g., Falwell and Jeffress) are hard to square with the Bible, especially the teachings and example of Jesus. In his classic work *Christian Attitudes toward War and Peace*, church historian Roland Bainton observes that "one finds it difficult to call an ethic Christian which takes no account of the ethical precepts and principles of the New Testament. To be Christian an ethic must posit and seek to implement in proper balance love, justice, the integrity of the self, and the integrity of the other person—even should he be the enemy."[18] Bainton was a pacifist, but peace builders will agree with him that love, justice, and concern for the other matter, including in cases where that other person is an enemy. With this in mind, peace builders have a hard time considering the ethics of justified violence as Christian in any meaningful sense.

Early followers of Jesus internalized his teachings about nonviolence. They did not participate in the revolt against Rome in 66 CE. Instead, they chose to flee Jerusalem. Sentiments such as those expressed by Falwell and Jeffress are hard to square with the early church's interpretation of how they should live (at least before the conversion of the emperor Constantine in 312 CE).[19] For example, Justin Martyr argued that Christians should refuse to fight in war and should accept death as a witness to the truth. Athenagoras taught that Christians should be averse to violence and killing. Tertullian taught that Christians are clearly forbidden from using the sword by the teachings of Jesus. Cyprian was clearly opposed to the killing of human beings, both by the state and by individuals. Origen also defended pacifism in his writings. Finally, consider the words of Lactantius, right before Constantine's conversion:

> For when God forbids us to kill, He not only prohibits us from open violence, which is not even allowed by the public laws, but He warns us against the commission of those things which are esteemed lawful among men. . . . It makes no difference whether you put a man to death by word, or rather by the sword, since it is the act of putting to death itself which is prohibited. There-

fore, with regard to this precept of God, there ought to be no exception at all; but that it is always unlawful to put to death a man, whom God willed to be a sacred animal.[20]

While the views of the early church fathers are not intrinsically decisive, they are certainly worth considering. Augustine, who comes on to the scene after Constantine's conversion, believes there are such things as just wars and just executions by the state. Nevertheless, it is with sadness that Augustine admits that a good man may have to fight in a just war. He also believes the reality of war is rooted in human wickedness.[21] The attitudes of the early church fathers stand as a much-needed correction to those in our day who profess Christ but seem to relish violence, or at least the threat of it, against those they regard as enemies.

Peace building takes seriously the views of the early church. It has a strong presumption against, disdain for, and desire to avoid violence. It includes a strong presumption in favor of nonviolence. It also emphasizes the value of nonviolence as a response to persecution. There is a difference between choosing nonviolence when being persecuted for one's faith and choosing it when one is a potential crime victim. "One might choose nonresistance when suffering for Christ but choose to resist in a crime-oriented aggression for the sake of others or even for the sake of the aggressor himself. . . . The Christian should ask whether or not physical resistance is the only action available or whether there are other options such as talk or deception. . . . If there seems to be no other option but to resist with physical force, the Christian should discern whether killing is the only alternative or whether lesser violence would adequately restrain evil."[22] Peace builders will make these distinctions and will ask these questions. They do this to avoid violence and to minimize it when they deem it necessary.

Peace building takes the passages that pacifists often use in support of their views much more seriously than many of their opponents seem to. Yet, to be clear, there will be cases where the use of some forms of violence is justified in defense of oneself and others. In this way, peace building is a compromise position between just-war theory and pacifism.

Peace builders, in the sense I'm using the term, recognize that we have an obligation as Christians not to use violence. Nevertheless, there may be cases where "one has a higher obligation to defend oneself and one's family against the imminent threat of harm over and above the obligation not to use violence. This way of approaching the problem concedes that the pacifist has a valid point about the Bible prohibiting the use of violence. But nonviolence is not an absolute under this view and can be outweighed by the higher mandate to love one's neighbor as oneself."[23]

Some might be concerned about an ethical approach in which some obligations are considered to be stronger than others. But such thought is present in the Gospels. Jesus criticizes the scribes and Pharisees for being concerned about tithing spices but neglecting "the weightier matters of the law: justice and mercy and faith" (Matt. 23:23). In sum, peace builders agree that "fewer and fewer conditions or exceptions could apply to the normative ethic of nonviolence. This is not to say, however, that [Thomas Merton and the Dalai Lama] deny absolutely the possibility of justifiably using violent force."[24]

Given the above, peace builders don't merely ask, "Is violence justified here?" They consider more important questions, such as, "How can I (or we) avoid violence, even if it is justified?" "Is this a case where it is the will of God that I sacrifice my life, or refuse to use violence even in defense of others?" "What can be done to reduce (or even eliminate) violence?"

Even if, in a particular situation, violence is justified according to just-war theory or the justified violence view, Christians ultimately must let their lives and choices be shaped by Christ, as the Holy Spirit guides. And this means that peace building endorses the belief that *there may be times when a Christian should allow his own life, and even the lives of those he loves, to be taken.* I agree, then, with Charles Marsh, quoted at the beginning of this chapter. Christians need not be uniformly pacifist, but it is nevertheless true that "the religion of Jesus clusters undeniably around the practices of forgiveness, reconciliation, and the preferential option for nonviolence."[25]

Guns and the Gospel of Jesus Christ

It is time to directly address Charles Marsh's question, "How might members of the body of Christ think more faithfully about guns and gun violence in light of Christian peculiarity and the doctrine of the Kingdom of God?"

The good news of the gospel is not merely that our sins can be forgiven. The good news of the gospel includes this but involves much more.[26] The gospel is the good news that God is making himself and his kingdom available to us now. It is available to everyone. It is something, if we so choose, to be entered into now. Those who entrust themselves to God are not accepting a future kingdom to be enjoyed later but are choosing to enter into that kingdom now. When they love God with all that they are, and their neighbors as themselves, and abide in Christ, it will be "natural" to seek justice and the common good. The kingdom of God is not a theocracy, nor is it a social or political program. God's kingdom is, simply, "the range of his effective will, where what he wants done is done."[27] Many distinct social or political programs might reflect God's will. The kingdom of God is not a violent kingdom; it does not advance by force. In fact, the kingdom of God, in its fullness, will have no room for animosity or violence but rather is "righteousness and peace and joy in the Holy Spirit" (Rom. 14:17).

When Christians pray, "Your kingdom come, your will be done, on earth as it is in heaven" (see Matt. 6:10), they are praying for a world where gun violence is eradicated. "The kingdom of God consists of peace with justice, of life unmarred by killing."[28] This goal will not be fully reached until the kingdom comes in its fullness, when there are a new heaven and a new earth, when we live in a community of love with the Trinity at its center. Then, God

> will wipe every tear from their eyes.
> Death will be no more;
> mourning and crying and pain will be no more.
>
> (Rev. 21:4)

But just because such violence will not be eliminated until then, it does not follow that we cannot make significant progress toward that goal. As followers of Christ, we should work to make such progress a reality.

As a *Christianity Today* editorial points out, violence arrived early on the scene in Genesis 4, when Cain killed Abel.[29] Two chapters later, violence is said to be ubiquitous on the earth. God's hatred of violence is found in the prophets (Ezek. 8:17; Hos. 12:1; Obad. 10). The editorial goes on to argue that given God's hatred of violence, and given the prevalence of violence in the United States, some gun regulations are needed.

But God's hatred of violence is not just in Genesis and the prophets. It can also be found in Psalms and Proverbs and throughout the Old Testament.[30]

What about the New Testament? As Richard Hays, a New Testament scholar, observes, "From Matthew to Revelation, we find a consistent witness against violence and a calling to the community to follow the example of Jesus in *accepting* suffering rather than *inflicting* it."[31]

It would take at least an entire book, and likely more than that, to engage in a comprehensive study of all that the Bible has to say about violence. (For those readers interested in looking at this in more detail, see the various references in the notes.)

In some situations Jesus clearly rejects the use of violence as a means of advancing the kingdom of God. In Luke 9, as he begins his journey to Jerusalem to be crucified, people in a Samaritan village reject him. When the apostles James and John find out about this, they say to Jesus, "Lord, do you want us to command fire to come down from heaven and consume them?" But Jesus "turned and rebuked them" (Luke 9:54-55). In John 18:36, Jesus replies to Pilate's questioning with the words, "My kingdom is not from this world. If my kingdom were from this world, my followers would be fighting to keep me from being handed over to the Jews. But as it is, my kingdom is not from here."

In Matthew 26:47-54, Judas leads a crowd to the garden in order to betray Jesus. Peter draws his sword and cuts off the ear of the high priest's slave. Jesus tells him to put his sword away, "for all who take the sword will perish by the sword" (v. 52). In Luke's account (Luke 22:47-53), Jesus proceeds to heal the injured slave. Wayne Grudem argues that Jesus is not prohibiting all violence in this passage. Instead, Jesus is ensuring that nothing stands between himself and the cross. He's making sure that the disciples don't instigate a violent revolt against the Romans. More generally, "Jesus did not want Peter to try to advance the kingdom of God by force."[32] For Grudem, this is why he tells Peter to put his sword away and why he says that "all who take the sword will perish by the sword."

Grudem claims that Jesus does not want Peter to use violence *to advance God's kingdom*. As Christians, *all that we do* should ultimately be for the sake of God's glory and kingdom. Given this, it would follow for Grudem that neither Peter nor we should engage in acts of violence, for any purpose. This is a problem for Grudem's interpretation, as his argument for the view seems to contradict the view itself.

God's heart is with the marginalized and the downtrodden. As James 1:27 states, "Religion that is pure and undefiled before God, the Father, is this: to care for orphans and widows in their distress, and to keep oneself unstained by the world" (see also Isa. 10:1-3; 32:15-18; 60:17-18). James 1 arguably applies to anyone who is marginalized in a society, anyone who suffers due to poverty, injustice, or prejudice.

How is this relevant to gun violence? Guns are used to create widows and orphans. The more we can do to keep guns out of the hands of those who would kill, the better. Gun violence is a problem for those living in areas where poverty is prevalent. In addition, African Americans are sixteen times more likely to be homicide victims than non-Hispanic whites. Young men (ages fifteen to thirty-four) make up half of all murder victims. In this age group, homicide is the leading cause of death for African Americans, and the second-leading cause of death for Latinos. Of all murders in this age group, guns are used 84 percent of the time.[33]

Guns are also a problem in cases of domestic violence. For example, one study focused on pregnant women who were victims of abuse and living below the poverty line. If their abuser had access to a gun, the level of abuse was much higher.[34] More generally, the federal and state laws aimed at preventing violence against an intimate partner (or the child of an intimate partner) have helped to reduce these types of homicides. But more can be done. One in five victims of homicide is a woman, and for women the danger usually has to do with their spouses or intimate partners. A gun in the home makes it more likely that violence will escalate, and when it escalates to murder, the victim is usually the woman.[35] These facts alone should move followers of Christ to see what can be done to prevent such suffering and death, including restrictions on who can own a gun and what type of gun can be possessed.

As mentioned above, perhaps the most widely cited passage of the Bible to support nonviolence comes from the Sermon on the Mount:

> "You have heard that it was said, 'An eye for an eye and a tooth for a tooth.' But I say to you, Do not resist an evildoer. But if anyone strikes you on the right cheek, turn the other also. . . . You have heard that it was said, 'You shall love your neighbor and hate your enemy.' But I say to you, Love your enemies and pray for those who persecute you, so that you may be children of your Father in heaven." (Matt. 5:38–39, 43–44)

Grudem's view of the passage limits its scope in a way that allows for using violence in self-defense and defense of others. Many think Jesus prohibited self-defense when he told people to turn the other cheek. However, Grudem argues that this passage does no such thing. Rather, it prohibits us from taking vengeance, from retaliating against those who have insulted us. He argues that being struck (or slapped) on the right cheek, as the passage describes, would have been done with the back of the right hand as an insult. The point, then, is that the follower of Christ should not strike back when struck as an insult. The context, according to Grudem, has nothing to do with defending oneself or others against harm or attempted murder. He contends that in the Sermon on the Mount, this and other statements are not absolute commands but rather examples of Christlike conduct. They are not necessarily to be obeyed in every situation. He goes on to argue that failing to defend oneself (or presumably one's neighbor) against a violent attack often leads to more harm and more wrongdoing. It follows that stopping an attack before harm is done is a way to love one's neighbor as oneself. The same applies to one's enemies. It is loving to stop them from perpetrating an attack.[36]

In his explanation of Matthew 5:38-48, Hays argues that the primary point of the passage is that Christians are to display nonviolent love for their enemies.[37] In Matthew's Gospel, the Sermon on the Mount is Jesus's explanation of what the kingdom of God is like, and of the life that it demands of his followers. It is a life in which anger and lust are overcome, marital fidelity is preserved, language is truthful, retaliation is rejected, and enemies are loved rather than hated. This way of life is to be the mark of the disciples of Jesus. It is their obligation to teach it to all who would follow him (Matt. 28:16-20). For Hays, nonviolent love of enemies is a command to be obeyed and "a symbolic pointer to the character of the peaceful city set on a hill."[38] Jesus practiced it. So should his followers.

To those who claim that being struck on the right cheek signifies an insult, Hays argues that nothing in the context points to this type of scenario. In fact, such arguments are made "on the basis of an arbitrary assumption that a blow on the right cheek could be delivered only with the back of the adversary's hand." The action required of the follower of Jesus, turning the other cheek, symbolizes a rejection of physical retaliation to physical attack. The vision of God's kingdom is one in which the disciples of Jesus "bear witness to another reality . . . a reality in which peacefulness, service, and generosity are valued above self-defense and personal rights."[39] Hays goes on to argue that this interpretation is consistent with the rejection of violence in the other Gospels, Acts, Paul's letters, Hebrews, 1 Peter, James, Revelation, and indeed the entire New Testament.

The peace builder view of the passage, which I favor, agrees that many of the teachings of the Sermon on the Mount are not absolute commands. It differs from pacifism in that it allows for cases in which violence might be justified. But it differs from the justified violence view because it has a much narrower view of when violence is justified.

In his discussion of the Sermon on the Mount, Dallas Willard argues that we should interpret it as a sermon, as a work that develops one line of thought that should guide how we interpret it.[40] The main point of the sermon is to explain the kingdom of God into which Jesus is calling us. It is not a set of laws. It offers illustrations of what life in the kingdom is like, what a life of love, power, truth, and grace under the rule of God is. More specifically, it reveals to us what the kingdom heart, a human heart submitted to God and his kingdom, looks like in the everyday situations and challenges of human existence.

In his discussion of Matthew 5:38-48, Willard points out that the focus is on personal injuries and not on evils at a larger social level.[41] Because of this, he thinks applying the passage to war and other social evils is a mistake. The follower of Jesus, as a citizen of God's kingdom, will choose to remain vulnerable in the face of a personal insult, injury, or imposition. His followers "will not take their defense into their own hands and do whatever is necessary to protect themselves."[42] Their characteristic response will be to allow others to injure them, without injuring them in response. This does not mean they will not defend someone else who is vulnerable; we are to turn our own cheek, not someone else's. But to be clear, Jesus is not setting down a law to be followed in every situation, regardless of circumstances. Instead, he is illustrating what his followers will predictably and characteristically do in such situations. There will be times when his followers do not turn the other cheek, but such situations will be very rare. It is up to us to determine if vulnerability is appropriate. As Willard puts it,

> If turning the other cheek means I will then be dead, or that others will suffer great harm, I have to consider this larger context. Much more than my personal pain or humiliation is involved. Does that mean I will "shoot first"? Not necessarily, but it means I can't just invoke a presumed "law of required vulnerability." I must decide before God what to do, and there may be grounds for some measure of resistance . . . the grounds will never be personal retaliation. . . . In every concrete situation we have to

ask ourselves, not "Did I do the specific things in Jesus' illustrations?" but "Am I being the kind of person Jesus' illustrations are illustrations of?"[43]

I believe that Willard's views about the Sermon on the Mount in general and Matthew 5:38-48, in particular, support peace building. Both recognize that while there can be exceptions to the ideal of nonviolence, those exceptions will be very rare. A disciple of Jesus should be characterized by seeking peace and avoiding violence, just as he was.

So, what are the implications of the gospel for guns and gun violence? Consider three lessons that can be drawn from the above discussion of peace building and the gospel.

First, too many who advocate a justified violence view and apply it to guns seem trigger-happy with respect to violence, both literally and figuratively. If we ask ourselves whether we are being true to the teachings of Christ, whether our hearts reflect the reality of his kingdom, anything less than a strong presumption against the use of violence, including the use of a gun in a violent act, is unacceptable. Violence is not to be celebrated, exalted, or glorified. We are to do all we can to seek peace, to build peace, and to bring about justice through peaceful means.

Second, followers of Jesus must make sure that guns do not become idols, false gods in whom they wrongly place their trust for safety and security. This does not mean that if one has a gun, it is necessarily an idol. Nevertheless, our ultimate trust in all matters, including those involving safety and security, life and death, should be in God. We must take care that we are exemplifying the character of Christ and growing more deeply in his virtues.

Third, given the depravity of the human heart, we should do all we can to make it more difficult for those who would use a gun to harm the innocent to gain access to one. This includes people who suffer from a dangerous form of mental illness, people under the age of twenty-one, people with substance abuse issues, and those guilty of domestic violence or who are under some sort of restraining order. These suggestions will be discussed and defended in more detail in the final chapter. It is simply too easy to buy a gun in the

United States, both legally and illegally. The fact that human beings are sinful supports the claim that more laws, and better-enforced laws, should be in place. As Romans 13:1–7 tells us, one of the functions of government is to restrain evil. One way this can be done is by making it more difficult for people who should not have access to firearms to gain such access. We can enact and enforce laws that will allow responsible gun owners to possess firearms while at the same time reducing the number of irresponsible and dangerous people with guns.

Guns in Church?

Should we bring guns to church? Falwell and Jeffress think so. If some companies have their way, we'll bring guns to church to protect all that we hold dear:

> In the February 2018 issue of Guns magazine, a full-page advertisement by Crossbreed Holster reflects the gun industry's recognition of the new market. A thirty-something man in a tweed jacket and dress jeans holds a little girl's hand—a blue bow has been neatly tied in her long auburn hair—as the two walk to church. The red-brick sanctuary and its white spire appear in the short distance ahead. At first glance everything about the scene looks normal, until you notice the position of the man's/father's free hand. A magnified cutaway highlights the new Crossbreed Supertuck, a handsome handcrafted holster inside the waistband, which encases a Springfield XD-S handgun. "Proud to be on your side," a banner reads. The father's free hand is positioned for a quick retrieval of the weapon. Though there are no signs of visible danger, we know that evil lurks everywhere, evil men with guns. "This is the world we're living in," Pastor Jeffress said. And "we need to do everything we can" to protect ourselves, our families and our churches. Even if it means—as in the Supertuck ad—that carrying our guns to church requires leaving our Bibles behind.[44]

Gun violence at church is, unfortunately, a reality. There were 147 shootings at churches from 2006 to 2016, more than the 137 that occurred between 1980 and 2005.[45] In recent years, there have been deadly mass shootings at churches.

On June 17, 2015, a twenty-one-year-old white supremacist shot and killed nine people at the Emanuel AME Church in Charleston, South Carolina. The shooter was arrested the next day and sentenced to death in January of 2017. He expressed no remorse at his trial. Mike Huckabee claimed that if only someone at the prayer meeting had a concealed-carry permit and was carrying a gun, the shooting could have been prevented, or at least the carnage could have been reduced.[46]

On November 5, 2017, a twenty-six-year-old man entered the First Baptist Church of Sutherland Springs, Texas, and killed twenty-six people during a Sunday morning service. A neighbor fired at the shooter as he left the church; the shooter later died of a self-inflicted gunshot wound to the head. In response to this, Texas attorney general Ken Paxton, as well as many pastors, argued that if churchgoers would arm themselves, as allowed by Texas law, then someone could stop a shooter before he does too much harm.[47]

This sort of response is standard for many gun-rights supporters. The answer to gun violence is more guns. We need more guns in school, more guns in the workplace, more guns at bars and nightclubs, more guns at shopping malls, and we need more guns in church. But is this right? The Reverend Michael McBride argues that this "is not the religion of Jesus. I think it is becoming increasingly apparent that we have a practice of blasphemous Christianity by many so-called Christians. Jesus is the Prince of Peace in a world of war. Rather than continue to push for more instruments of death, which are unable to keep us safe, we must rather start to call for a more peaceful existence that limits the proliferations of instruments of death. Any faith leader that calls for an opposite of that . . . has a deep moral hole in their soul, and they should be ignored."[48] Kevin Farrell, Roman Catholic bishop of the Diocese of Dallas, implemented rules prohibiting concealed handgun license holders from carrying guns on church property: "This policy is rooted in the belief that our churches, schools and other places of worship are intended to be sanctuaries—holy sites where people come to pray and participate in the ministry of the Church."[49] Or, as Shane Claiborne puts it, "Jesus carried a cross not a gun. He said greater love has no one than this—to lay down their life for another. The early Christians said 'for Christ we can die but we cannot kill.' When Peter picked up a sword to protect Jesus and cut off a guy's ear, Jesus scolded him and put the ear back on. The early Christians said 'when Jesus disarmed Peter he disarmed every Christian.' Evil is real but Jesus teaches us to fight evil without becoming evil. On the cross we see what love looks like when it stares evil in the face. Love is willing to die but not to kill."[50]

Who is right? Should we have guns in our midst, or should we keep weapons out of the sanctuary where we corporately worship the Prince of Peace? If we prohibit guns at church, are we being irresponsible, leaving ourselves and our children defenseless? Or are we fighting evil by becoming evil when we have guns in church? There are no easy answers.

A first option, the one practiced by the members of Robert Jeffress's church and of many others around the country, is to allow members with concealed-carry permits to bring their guns into church. This option should be rejected. In November 2017, during a discussion about allowing guns in church, a member of the First United Methodist Church in Tellico Plains, Tennessee, shared that he carried his gun with him everywhere. After showing the gun to others at the meeting, he put it back in his pocket. When another church member wanted to see the gun, it went off as the man again removed it from his pocket. The bullet hit his hand and his wife's abdomen and forearm.[51] In December of 2017, two teenage boys at a house attached to a church thought they heard an intruder at the church. One of the boys got a rifle and tripped over an extension cord, causing the gun to fire. The bullet struck the other boy in the chest, killing him. If bringing weapons to church becomes more common, accidents will become more common as well.[52]

People tend to overestimate their own abilities to respond well in a crisis, such as a mass shooting. Imagine a lone gunman entering a sanctuary and five, ten, or twenty-five people trying to stop him with their guns. The chances of chaos and harm are increased by the presence of multiple guns in such situations. Even those who have received extensive training, such as police officers and soldiers, make mistakes in life-threatening circumstances. Humility counsels those without such training to accept their own limitations, and also to admit to the chance that they would do more harm than good in an active shooter situation.

A second option is to have trained security personnel or off-duty police officers provide security. Some churches pay to have a visible off-duty police officer at their building every Sunday; they quote studies that show that a police presence is a deterrent. One pastor whose church does this advised those who can't get local police help to hire a security guard and to make sure that person is visible.[53]

A final option, then, is to prohibit the presence of guns in or around church, carried by either members or trained personnel. This decision is guided by the conviction that weapons do not belong in a worship service. It seeks to demonstrate the strength and vulnerability of nonviolent resistance. It also seeks to exemplify peace by its rejection of violence.

Only the second and third options are viable. Armed church members, even with concealed-carry permits, are generally not equipped to handle the stress of an active shooter situation. And the more guns in church, the greater the chances that accidental shootings might happen. Regardless of whether a church hires an off-duty police officer or private security, allows members to carry guns into its services, or does none of the above, there is one thing on which we should all be able to agree. Followers of Jesus should be working toward a world in which the risk of being a victim of a shooting anywhere, including a mass shooting at church, is minimized. If the primary response is to arm ourselves at church, then we are not being faithful to our calling as ambassadors for Christ (2 Cor. 5:20). Our enemies are not flesh and blood, they are spiritual (Eph. 6:10–20). I am concerned that we forget these and many other important truths in our impulse to answer gun violence merely with more guns, especially in our houses of worship.

Erik Grayson, a Methodist pastor in North Charleston, South Carolina, has a no-guns policy at his church. But for him, it is about more than policy; it is about what it means to be a disciple of Jesus: "I want to bring people to a deeper understanding of what it means to be the body of Christ. It's not just about me saying 'No guns.' I want this to be something that's formative and will teach people to really reflect upon what it means to follow Jesus as a church."[54]

Whatever denominations and individual churches decide on this issue, Grayson's point is well taken. We must all reflect on what it means to follow Jesus as his church. Such reflection, rather than fear or a desire to be in control, must guide our choices.

Conclusion

Christians have been thinking about war and violence and what it means to be faithful in this fallen world since the time of Christ. We have not yet reached a consensus. Many advocate, sometimes fiercely, for justified violence. Others reject this view and argue for pacifism in both the political and personal realms.

We've seen that there is a third way. Peace building keeps the future Christian hope of peace and tranquillity as a guiding truth for life in the present. There is a future in which wars and violence will cease:

> Many peoples shall come and say,
> "Come, let us go up to the mountain of the LORD,
>   to the house of the God of Jacob;
>   that he may teach us his ways
>   and that we may walk in his paths."
> For out of Zion shall go forth instruction,
>   and the word of the LORD from Jerusalem.
> He shall judge between the nations,
>   and shall arbitrate for many peoples;
>   they shall beat their swords into plowshares,
>   and their spears into pruning hooks;

nation shall not lift up sword against nation,
    neither shall they learn war any more. (Isa. 2:3–4)

Peace builders believe we should do all we can to realize this hope now, even though it will not be fully realized until the redemption of all at the end of the age. They are realists about the presence of violence in a fallen world. But they choose hope over despair, optimism over pessimism, and they seek to eliminate as much violence as they can until that hope is, finally, fulfilled.

5

A BIBLE AND A GUN

Johnny Cash, with a little help from U2, sings the following lines in "The Wanderer":

> I went out walking,
> with a Bible and a gun,
> The word of God lay heavy on my heart,
> I was sure I was the one.

For many in the United States, the Bible and a gun symbolize faith and patriotism. I've seen T-shirts with a picture of a Bible and a gun with the following words: "Two things every American needs to know that they don't teach in school." Or, consider the following slogan on a bumper sticker:

> Gun-Totin'
> Bible-Clingin'
> American on Board

Despite the curious marriage of these two powerful symbols, modern technologies do not, of course, appear in the Bible. Guns and email are not found on the pages of Scripture. However, the Bible does mention weapons and the extraordinary violence they can bring. Prominent examples include swords (Gen. 34:25; Isa. 34:5–6; Eph. 6:17; Rev. 1:16), spears (Num. 25:6–8; 2 Sam. 2:23), slings (1 Sam.

17:40; Judg. 20:16), and arrows (Lam. 3:12–13; Eph. 6:16). These primitive weapons were the warp and woof of ancient war and conflict.

Despite the distance of time and place, some specific biblical passages have been used to support gun use and gun ownership.

Not Peace but a Sword

Jesus's own words sound like an endorsement of violence. In Matthew 10:34, Jesus says, "Do not think that I have come to bring peace to the earth. I have not come to bring peace, but a sword" (ESV). Luke 12:51 puts it differently, "Do you think that I have come to bring peace to the earth? No, I tell you, but rather division!" (CEB). Taken out of context, these verses could be slogans for owning weapons. For example, the Conservative Christians of Alabama's website includes an article entitled "Gun Control and the Bible" in which Matthew 10:34 is cited as a biblical justification for opposing gun control.[1]

However, these passages have a context, both broad and narrow. Immediately following the cited words of Jesus in Matthew 10, he expounds on what he means, saying:

> "For I have come to set a man against his father,
>   and a daughter against her mother,
>   and a daughter-in-law against her mother-in-law;
>   and one's foes will be members of one's own household.

"Whoever loves father or mother more than me is not worthy of me; and whoever loves son or daughter more than me is not worthy of me; and whoever does not take up the cross and follow me is not worthy of me. Those who find their life will lose it, and those who lose their life for my sake will find it." (Matt. 10:35–39)

It seems clear that Jesus's point has nothing to do with using a sword to injure or kill others. Rather, his point is that we must be willing to give up our most important family relationships, if necessary, in order to faithfully follow him. His followers are to value

Jesus above all else. Choosing to follow him may bring division in our most cherished relationships.

In the culture of Jesus's hearers, his words were especially shocking. They challenged some deeply held beliefs about the family. Households at that time often included not just the immediate nuclear family but also other relatives. They would live near one another, perhaps sharing a courtyard with other married sons and their families. Married sons tended not to leave. They and their families were embedded in the larger family group. And the honor of this group, the extended family, was very important. Jesus's point is that the honor and unity of a family extended beyond the nuclear family. Given this, his words in Matthew 10 (and Luke 12) would have challenged the central values of family continuity, tradition, stability, and unity.

This passage makes several points.[2] First, Jesus is telling the disciples that family members who do not also become followers of Christ may oppose them. Second, Jesus is more important than the approval of one's own family (or even of receiving civil treatment from them!). Finally, Jesus is calling those who follow him to love him not only more than their own families but also more than their very lives. It is difficult to use this passage as justification for arming oneself with a sword or a gun.

Violence and the Cleansing of the Temple by Jesus (John 2:13-22)

Jesus's cleansing of the temple is often mentioned to justify the use of violence. Each of the four Gospels includes an account of his disruption of the temple (Matt. 21:12-17; Mark 11:15-18; Luke 19:45-46; and John 2:13-22). Here, we will primarily focus on John's account:

> The Passover of the Jews was near, and Jesus went up to Jerusalem. In the temple he found people selling cattle, sheep, and doves, and the money changers seated at their tables. Making a whip of cords, he drove all of them out of the temple, both the

sheep and the cattle. He also poured out the coins of the money changers and overturned their tables. He told those who were selling the doves, "Take these things out of here! Stop making my Father's house a marketplace!" His disciples remembered that it was written, "Zeal for your house will consume me." The Jews then said to him, "What sign can you show us for doing this?" Jesus answered them, "Destroy this temple, and in three days I will raise it up." The Jews then said, "This temple has been under construction for forty-six years, and will you raise it up in three days?" But he was speaking of the temple of his body. After he was raised from the dead, his disciples remembered that he had said this; and they believed the scripture and the word that Jesus had spoken.

Some take this passage to show that violence is permissible because Jesus himself engaged in an act of violence. They claim that Jesus fashioned a whip and used it against animals and people, forcefully driving them out of the temple. In Mark's account, Jesus also prohibits anyone from carrying anything through the temple area—perhaps using force to accomplish this. In their book *An Introduction to Biblical Ethics*, Robertson McQuilkin and Paul Copan discuss this passage as part of a section on war and peace. They argue that the New Testament is not nonmilitaristic and state that "Jesus used force in driving moneychangers from the temple and (forcibly?) stopping merchants from entering the temple."[3] However, there is some ambiguity here. Force comes in many varieties. One might use force without harming anyone. No one is reported being harmed or injured by what Jesus does in the temple.

There are numerous interpretations of Jesus's actions in the temple.[4] Many in the early church interpreted what Jesus did as physically nonviolent. Augustine, however, argues that it provides a moral justification for violence by Christians against heretics and those who would divide the church. Many Christians follow Augustine's lead and use this passage to widen the scope of the forms and targets of violence. Over the centuries, this belief became deeply entrenched in the Christian tradition. As Andy Alexis-Baker puts it:

Since antiquity, theologians and church leaders have cited the temple incident for many purposes, including condemning usury and greed, critiquing merchants, promoting anti-Semitism, and calling for inner conversion. Perhaps the most ubiquitous use of the temple incident, however, has been to justify Christian violence. From just war to Crusades to executing heretics, Jesus' action in the temple has provided fuel for righteous violence and killing.[5]

He adds that because John's account is the only one in which the whip appears, it has played (and still does play) a central role for many who seek to justify violence from a Christian perspective.

But is this correct? Does the cleansing of the temple by Jesus truly justify at least some forms of Christian violence? Is violent action an acceptable response to WWJD?

As noted above, the passage contains ambiguities. Yet, a solid case can be made that this passage does not justify violence. More importantly, related to the topic of this book, it is certain that this passage cannot be used to justify using a weapon to injure or kill someone. Careful attention to context, historical and literary, is crucial. The temple itself covered roughly thirty-five acres of space.[6] The outer courtyard was the largest and most open part of the temple area. People could exchange money to get the accepted currency and could purchase animals to use for sacrifices. The incident did not occur in a small enclosed area, but instead: "we need to envision him creating as much commotion as one man could manage in a few minutes' time in one portion of the open space in a complex encompassing about five or six city blocks, with hundreds of people coming and going. *Most visitors to the temple that day would never have noticed it.*"[7] Many conclude that what Jesus is doing here is symbolic, something like what a Hebrew prophet might do in order to show and teach the values of God.

But was it a violent act? Many scholars argue that it was not. To see why, we must consider some details in John's account. The Greek term *phragellion*, often translated as "whip" in the passage, could refer to a scourge (an instrument of torture or punishment), a whip, or even a lash. Translations differ: "scourge of small cords" (KJV);

"whip out of cords" (NIV); "whip from ropes" (CEB). So, what did Jesus use? Evidence indicates that weapons were not allowed in the temple area. Apparently, Jesus made the "whip of cords/ropes" from materials that were on hand. He likely would have employed material used in animal bedding, fodder, or ropes used to tie up animals. If so, this was nothing like the Roman instrument of torture, both in its makeup and in the potential harm it could cause.

Also, did Jesus use the makeshift whip on animals, people, both, or neither? The NRSV apparently takes "all" to refer only to animals: "Making a whip of cords, he drove all of them out of the temple, both the sheep and the cattle." Many other translations follow suit (ASV, NIV, and TNIV). The text does not describe what Jesus did in the temple as a *justification* for violent acts against people. In addition, a makeshift whip made out of rope seems barely capable of inflicting violence on the cattle and sheep, as it "would hardly do much more than get them moving out the door, their owners running after them to keep them from running amok."[8] Thus, Jesus would in effect have been shooing animals out of the temple precincts.[9] Only John's Gospel mentions a whip, and only John's Gospel mentions the animals. It makes sense, then, to see the makeshift whip as the means of shooing animals out of the area. It seems to be quite a stretch to use this episode as justification for inflicting physical harm on other human beings.

What applications might the temple cleansing hold for us? First, nothing in the accounts of this event indicate that ethical principles are to be drawn from it. Rather, the temple cleansing tells us something about the identity of Jesus as the Christ.[10] But, of course, Jesus is our exemplar, our role model, and so we cannot too easily dismiss the claim that there are ethical implications here, even if they are not the main point of the passage. But what might they be, related to our focus in this book?

There is a significant logical gap between what Jesus did in the temple and warfare, capital punishment, and use of a gun. Even if he did strike some people with the makeshift whip, the difference between that and killing another person, even in self-defense, is noteworthy. A passage that does not involve an act of killing, the inflicting of serious injury, or, as far as we can tell, an injury of any kind to an animal or a person cannot be used to justify such acts.

While there are a range of interpretations of the temple incident, ultimately the passage itself does not justify Christian violence. In fact, the accounts in the four canonical Gospels show remarkable restraint, both in the action and the narrative.[11] As David Rensberger concludes, "The traditional understanding of Jesus's action in the temple area as an act of violent fury cannot be sustained on a careful reading of the Gospels."[12] The accounts have so many gaps. The temptation is to fill those gaps as we see fit. A violent Jesus is less countercultural for us, because he responds as we likely would, or as our own cultural idea of the masculine action hero would. Our "commonsense" reading of the passage here reveals what might be wrong with our common sense, rather than a Jesus who resorts to violence in order to accomplish his mission.

The most important point for our purposes is this: the zeal Jesus demonstrates for the temple does not justify injuring or killing anyone, *because nobody was injured or killed*. Clearly, then, it does not justify the use of a gun to injure or kill anyone today. There may be passages that justify or at least permit this or other forms of violence, but this passage is not one of them. To use it to justify arming oneself or harming others is to misuse and misapply the deeds of Jesus.

Worse Than an Unbeliever (1 Timothy 5:8)

In the documentary The *Armor of Light*, there is a scene in which Rev. Rob Schenck discusses with a group of Ohio pastors a hypothetical situation in which an innocent child is being forced into a car by a criminal and whether a Christian is obligated to save the child. The lesson here, for these pastors, is that such situations support the view that followers of Jesus should, or at least may, carry and use a gun. Schenck comments that he is surprised at the role of guns in their lives, in their thinking, and even in their spirituality.

One of the men in this discussion uses the Bible to justify his beliefs about why gun ownership and use are obligatory: "The Bible is very plain that a man who doesn't protect his wife and kids is worse than an infidel."[13] This appears to be a reference to 1 Timothy 5:1-8:

> Do not speak harshly to an older man, but speak to him as to a father, to younger men as brothers, to older women as mothers, to younger women as sisters—with absolute purity. Honor widows who are really widows. If a widow has children or grandchildren, they should first learn their religious duty to their own family and make some repayment to their parents; for this is pleasing in God's sight. The real widow, left alone, has set her hope on God and continues in supplications and prayers night and day; but the widow who lives for pleasure is dead even while she lives. Give these commands as well, so that they may be above reproach. And whoever does not provide for relatives, and especially for family members, has denied the faith and is worse than an unbeliever.

I have given the entire passage because, as usual, the context is crucial for understanding the intended meaning and applications of this passage. First Timothy has traditionally been understood as a letter from Paul to Timothy written in order to encourage and instruct him in his role as a teacher in the church, and to describe the functions and obligations of different people within it. After discussing the specific role of a teacher, Paul turns to the obligations that believers have to one another in Christ.

What is the point of verse 8: "And whoever does not provide for relatives, and especially for family members, has denied the faith and is worse than an unbeliever"? The language is strong and would have surely caught the attention of the first readers (or hearers). The primary point of the passage is that family members are obligated to care for their widowed relatives. Later in the chapter, in verse 16, Paul emphasizes this. He states that "If any believing woman has relatives who are really widows, let her assist them; let the church not be burdened, so that it can assist those who are real widows."

The intended application has to do with who should care for widows and other relatives who are in need and unable to provide for themselves. The point is that there should be an economic safety net for such people. Those who have relatives should receive help from them; those who are truly alone and have no one to come to their aid will depend on the church to meet their needs. Given that this is the actual subject of the passage, it is difficult to see how it justifies or obligates gun ownership and use.

But perhaps this is too quick. Can the application of this passage, and the particular verse in question, be extended in the way that the pastor from Ohio claims? The argument might be something along the following lines. We are obligated to provide for our family members. One way to provide for our family members is to protect them from harm. Sometimes the only way to protect them from harm is with a gun. We should have a gun to protect our family members from harm, if the need arises to do so.

However, in fairness, this interpretation strays too far from the actual passage. The scope of the passage is financial support, not the use of violence for defending someone who is being attacked. This is clear in the passage, and the scope is made even clearer when Paul instructs his readers that "If any believing woman has relatives who are really widows, let her assist them; let the church not be burdened, so that it can assist those who are real widows." There is no reference in the verse, passage, chapter, or letter to the use of violence in protection of others. The pastor from Ohio, and others who use this verse in this way, are guilty of reading too much into the Scripture, rather than taking it on its own terms. Whatever biblical justification there is for defending one's family with a weapon, it is not to be found here. To use it to justify arming oneself or harming others is to misuse and misapply the words of 1 Timothy.

A Cheerful Acceptance of Theft (Hebrews 10:32–34)

An analysis of data from the National Crime Victimization Survey from 2007 to 2011 shows that using a gun in self-defense is rare and does not reduce the likelihood of injury during a crime. In fact, the analysis shows that people in homes without a gun are not at any greater risk of becoming victims of theft, assault, or homicide by a criminal than people in homes with a gun. When a gun is in the home, the chance is greater that someone in that household will be shot by accident or die by homicide or suicide. However, guns are effective for protecting property:

> Guns did seem beneficial in one category: protecting against loss of property. Looking only at crimes in which the intent was to steal, the victim lost property in only 38% of the incidents when using a gun, compared with 56% of the incidents when taking other actions. But using some other weapon—Mace, for instance—appeared equally effective as using a gun.[14]

For Christians, however, justifying the use of violence, including the use of a gun, for the sake of protecting property is not an option. Many point to the teachings of Jesus in the Sermon on the Mount, where he tells his followers that if anyone wants to take their coat, they should also give that person their cloak (Matt. 5:40). A more directly relevant passage for our current question is Hebrews 10:32–34:

> But recall those earlier days when, after you had been enlightened, you endured a hard struggle with sufferings, sometimes being publicly exposed to abuse and persecution, and sometimes being partners with those so treated. For you had compassion for those who were in prison, and you cheerfully accepted the plundering of your possessions, knowing that you yourselves possessed something better and more lasting.

This is a challenging passage. Hebrews 10 describes the confidence believers have before God because of what Christ has done. They're urged to endure, to persevere in faith through suffering. One type of suffering they not only endured but also cheerfully accepted was the theft of their possessions. This cheerful acceptance was based on their confidence in "something better and more lasting." This is a description of their behavior and attitude in trying circumstances, but it is also an example for us to follow. Moreover, a more general respect for the value of life—the inherent dignity that humans possess as image bearers of God—supports the view that we should not use a gun to defend our property. The value of mere material possessions never outweighs the value of a human being's life, any human being's life.

This can be difficult to put into practice. There are many situations in which we cannot know the intent of those trying to take our property. Is that all they intend to do, or do they also intend to harm us or our loved ones? If the latter, this raises other issues that have already been discussed concerning self-defense and defense of others. Nevertheless, it is important to see that seeking to justify owning and using a gun to protect one's property is a nonstarter for followers of Jesus. Using a gun for this purpose may be an American value, but it isn't a Christian one.

The One Who Has No Sword (Luke 22:35–38)

One of the favorite New Testament proof texts used to justify owning and using a gun is Luke 22:35–38. In a debate I had with Ron Gleason on the subject of guns and gun laws, he concluded his reply to my case as follows: "Finally, Austin's article suffers from many vagaries and much one-sidedness. He cites Matthew 5:38–48 and Luke 9:51–56, but I find Luke 22:36–38 applicable."[15] Some Christian defenders of the right to own and use a gun argue that Luke 22:35–38 justifies owning and using a weapon, for both self-defense and defense of those vulnerable to violence.

Before we examine the passage, consider the following argument concerning a Christian worldview and the Second Amendment:

> Swords were used to kill people in Jesus' day. Did Jesus rail against the presence of swords and demand that no one but soldiers should carry them? No, in fact, he told His disciples that he who had no sword should buy one because of the troubled days ahead. Peter was carrying his sword in the garden when Jesus was arrested. While Jesus kept Peter from interfering with His arrest, Jesus did not use that situation to initiate a "sword control" campaign. Perhaps a more sensible way to control gun violence would be to encourage law-abiding citizens to carry

weapons, particularly in public areas. This approach creates a deterrent against the insane, the criminal, and a future government gone amok.[16]

Jesus may not have railed against the presence of swords, and he did not tell Peter to get rid of his sword in this passage. But we must not forget that in Matthew's narration of the same story, Jesus told him, "Put your sword back into its place; for all who take the sword will perish by the sword" (Matt. 26:52). The lessons to be drawn from this passage are not as clear as many seem to think.

But what about Luke 22:35-38? Does it support the claim that Christians can own and use weapons for self-defense? Is it in fact applicable to this issue, in the way many believe?

Again, context is key. In this passage, prior to his arrest, Jesus tells the disciples to buy a sword if they don't have one:

> He said to them, "When I sent you out without a purse, bag, or sandals, did you lack anything?" They said, "No, not a thing." He said to them, "But now, the one who has a purse must take it, and likewise a bag. And the one who has no sword must sell his cloak and buy one. For I tell you, this scripture must be fulfilled in me, 'And he was counted among the lawless'; and indeed what is written about me is being fulfilled." They said, "Lord, look, here are two swords." He replied, "It is enough." (Luke 22:35-38)

There are three primary ways of interpreting this passage and then determining the possible implications it has for us today. Some take the instructions of Jesus to buy swords as a justification for having weapons for self-defense. Others see a symbolic warning to the disciples concerning what is to come. Still others interpret it as a fulfillment of prophecy.

The opening of the Gospel of Luke records a promise to Theophilus that the text that follows contains an account of the life, death, resurrection, and ascension of Jesus, so that Theophilus would know the truth about these things. The task of Luke's Gospel is "to reassure his readers of the place of the Gentiles in the new community and the role of Jesus in God's plan."[17]

In Luke 22:35-38, Jesus is speaking to his disciples during the Passover meal. This passage falls within the final section of this gospel, where Luke reveals how the death of Jesus was not the end but a new beginning. The mission of the disciples becomes clear, in light of what God has done in and through Christ. Given the importance of understanding this mission, a proper interpretation and application of this passage are significant.

The first primary way that some interpret this passage is as *a justification for arming oneself for the sake of self-defense*. The disciples will be traveling and vulnerable, and should have a weapon for protection. Wayne Grudem makes this argument in his discussion of this passage, arguing that "Jesus seemed to encourage his disciples to have swords for self-defense."[18] Grudem states that it was common for people to carry swords for self-defense against robbers or to defend others who came under attack. The passage reveals that Jesus allowed at least two of the disciples to carry swords. When Jesus says, "It is enough," the meaning is that two swords are enough for this purpose. No more are needed at present.

A second way of interpreting this passage is by seeing the instructions of Jesus to buy swords as *symbolic*. The idea is that Jesus was not literally commanding his followers to purchase swords but rather was making them aware of the suffering and afflictions to come. In their previous missionary journey, they were instructed to seek out hospitality, taking nothing for their journey (Luke 9). Now, however, Jesus instructs them to sell their cloak if need be in order to buy a sword. On the symbolic interpretation of this passage, Jesus is attempting to communicate to the disciples that, like him, they will soon face hostility. This type of warning is standard for such farewell speeches. The intention is to warn the disciples to be ready for opposition, animosity, and hostility. As Joel Green puts the point, "mention of the need to purchase a sword adds to this picture a metaphorical reference to the coming reality. The possibility that Jesus' followers are literally to respond to hostility with a sword—that is, with violence—is negated in Luke 22:49-51."[19] In this latter passage, a disciple cuts off the ear of a slave of the high priest with a sword. But Jesus rebukes him, healing the slave. In Luke 22, the disciples mistakenly take him literally. When Jesus says, "It is enough," he is expressing exasperation at their lack of understanding and ending the discussion on this topic.

The third primary way of interpreting Luke 22:35-38 is as *a fulfillment of prophecy*. There is much to commend this reading. If we read the passage in a straightforward manner, on its own terms, we can see that the point of Jesus's instructing his disciples to purchase swords is the fulfillment of prophecy.[20] After the instruction to buy a sword, Jesus goes on to say, "For I tell you, this scripture must be fulfilled in me, 'And he was counted among the lawless'; and indeed what is written about me is being fulfilled." The prophecy referred to here is from Isaiah 53:12. According to G. W. H. Lampe, Luke takes this passage to apply to Jesus, who is now "numbered with the transgressors," because his disciples are armed with swords. Since they are armed, they are now transgressors of the law. One will even use a sword later in the Garden of Gethsemane, as we have already seen. Two swords are "enough" to fulfill this prophecy.[21]

Earlier, in Luke 18:31, Jesus told his disciples that all that the prophets wrote about the Son of Man would be fulfilled. This places the passage in Luke 22 within a framework of the fulfillment of prophecy. More specifically, the reference to Isaiah 53:12 comes directly after the command to purchase swords. When Luke reports Jesus saying, "For I tell you, this scripture must be fulfilled in me," he is linking the prophecy with the instruction to buy swords. As Neville puts the point, the context shows that "Jesus' instruction to his disciples to purchase swords finds its rationale in the scriptural saying about the suffering servant being counted among the lawless ones."[22] This prophecy is fulfilled immediately by the response of the disciples that they have two swords, which are in their possession when Jesus is arrested in the garden.

In context, Jesus predicts the future betrayal of Judas, the denial of Peter, and the subsequent repentance of his apostles. Each of these predictions of Jesus is fulfilled, including the prophecy concerning the swords and his being numbered among the transgressors. In fact, verse 37 is in the present tense. It can be translated "what is written about me here and now is finding its fulfillment."[23] All the predictions, then, of Luke 22:21-38 are fulfilled in the passion narrative. When arrested, Jesus is counted among the lawless, among the transgressors. These points lend support to the prophetic interpretation.

But what about the self-defense interpretation? Is this passage in Luke applicable in this way? Does it support the claim that Christians can own and use weapons, for self-defense and perhaps other purposes as well? Recall our discussion of Luke 22:47-51 in chapter 4. After Peter cuts off the ear of the high priest's slave, Jesus tells him, "No more of this!" Jesus then heals the injured slave. For many, this shows that Jesus must not be advocating violence in Luke 22:35-38.

The prophetic interpretation is preferable and is the majority explanation among biblical scholars. The point is not that the disciples should purchase a weapon to use for violence against others or for self-protection.[24] Using this passage as a justification for those views is a mistake.

In sum, while many gun-rights advocates interpret Luke 22:35-38 as a justification for the status quo and a Christian right to self-arm, it is wrong to do so. Christian defenders of owning and using guns for such purposes will have to look elsewhere for scriptural support of their position. Using this passage to justify arming oneself is to misuse and misapply the words of Jesus.

Conclusion

We began the chapter with lyrics from Johnny Cash's "The Wanderer." We'll end on a similar note. Later in the song, Cash sings:

> I stopped outside a church house,
> Where the citizens like to sit,
> They say they want the kingdom,
> But they don't want God in it.

Many who profess to follow Christ don't really want God, and they don't really want the kingdom of God as revealed in Scripture. To a degree, this is true of all of us. We are all deeply impacted by the Fall, our disordered desires, and our immoral choices. However, in my own experience, many Christians seem to espouse views that are more reflective of one of the kingdoms of this world than of the kingdom of Jesus. We cannot see into each other's hearts and should not be quick to judge others. Nevertheless, we should all reflect on what sort of kingdom we want and what sort of kingdom we are seeking to advance, not only in the gun debates but in all of life. We must allow our hearts and minds to be permeated with what is true and seek to live our lives accordingly. Authentic faith in Jesus, the Prince of Peace, and a flourishing community require nothing less.

6

CHRIST, CHARACTER, AND A COLT .45

Character matters. Cultivating it, in reliance on God's transformative power and grace, is central to the faithful Christian life. Character is also often ignored in the gun debates. This is a serious mistake.

The kingdom of God is revolutionary in many ways. Central to that revolution is the transformation of character. Followers of Christ, united with Christ, are transformed by the renewing of their minds (Rom. 12:1-2). Their beliefs, attitudes, habits—indeed, their very souls—are made new.[1] This is a large emphasis in the Sermon on the Mount: Jesus came to offer such deep change. In Matthew 5, for example, Jesus teaches his followers that they are to refrain not only from murder but also from being angry with their brother or sister. Not only are they to refrain from committing adultery, they are to refrain from lust, or adultery of the heart. Not only are they to refrain from falsely swearing an oath, but they are to be honest in all that they say. These are not new laws to follow or commands to obey. Instead, they describe what a heart that is under the rule of God and his kingdom will be like. This puts our character front and center, and it makes transformation of our character in Christ central to what it means to follow him.[2]

If character is a central concern, and if the character of Jesus is our ideal, then we must ask ourselves an important question as we think about guns: If Jesus were physically present in the United States of America today as he was in Palestine two thousand years ago, would Jesus own a firearm? Would Jesus carry a gun? Would Jesus shoot at another human being?

An American Idol

In 2012, Lucy McBath lost her only son, Jordan. He was murdered in front of a Florida convenience store. Why? The shooter felt threatened because Jordan and his friends were playing their music too loud and wouldn't turn it down. Lucy is a committed follower of Jesus, and in the years since Jordan's death has become involved in the fight against gun violence. In 2018, she won a Georgia congressional seat. Lucy is also featured in a documentary, *The Armor of Light*. Her words are telling: "We have replaced God with our guns."[3] Rob Schenck, a conservative evangelical Christian whose changing views are chronicled in the film, was struck by these words. He considered whether American Christians had "begun to idolize guns in their power to save us from perceived threats to our lives—or worse, our way of life." Schenck goes on to observe that "a gun is something designed by a human being and sometimes even hand-tooled, at least to some degree, and when we entrust our lives to it, we essentially look to those hand-crafted instruments to save us. . . . By venerating the Second Amendment, we evangelicals were in danger of violating the Second Commandment."[4]

Are McBath and Schenck correct? Have guns become American idols? Barreled and bulleted shrines of an old icon: security? Often, the answer is yes. To see why, we must ask whether we are trusting in guns for things that we should rely on God to grant us. We need not look far to find evidence of gun idolatry. Executive vice president of the NRA, Warren Cassidy, once said of the NRA, "You would get a far better understanding if you approached us as if you were approaching one of the great religions of the world."[5] Charles Marsh, a former Southern Baptist who is still connected to conservative evangelical culture, observes that some speak of guns in ways that Christians often speak of God: "*guns mark me as a man freed from bondage. . . . With a gun, I gain power over people who may want to harm me or my family.*"[6]

In *America and Its Guns: A Theological Exposé*, James Atwood explains why he thinks some are guilty of worshiping guns, of making the gun into an American idol.[7] His claim isn't that all guns are idols or that all gun owners are idolatrous. Atwood concludes that guns are idols for some. He is right. Atwood describes telltale signs of gun idolatry. Guns are idols when gun rights are sacrosanct and nonnegotiable, and discussion about limits being placed upon them cannot be done in a calm and rational manner. If we *need* guns to make us believe that we are in control, to protect us from harm, to make us feel secure, then our guns have become idols.

At their root, idols offer a promise of power (or at least the appearance of power). Guns offer the power of feeling secure. They enable humans to wound and kill at a distance. In contrast, God often feels absent and silent. The power of prayer can seem impotent against the barrel of a gun. Human leaders fail us. In such circumstances, guns can become idols. They become our rock, our shield, our protector. Guns give us a sense of power. They make us feel safe from those we fear. But these are lies. A misplaced trust rests in the trigger.

Would Christ Carry a Gun?

Upon hearing the call of Jerry Falwell Jr. for students at Liberty University to carry guns and "end those Muslims," many wondered about the character of Falwell's Jesus. Too often the Jesus worshiped is the Jesus projected from the worshiper. It is no surprise that the so-called conservative Jesus differs radically from the so-called liberal Jesus. The actual character of Christ matters. Christ is the question.

Shane Claiborne and Michael Martin argue that Jesus carried a cross, not a gun.[8] He told us to love our enemies, not kill them. He scolded Peter for drawing and using a sword. When he told Peter to put the sword away, Jesus was disarming every Christian. Christians, then, should follow in the steps of the Savior. The love of Jesus means his followers "would rather die with a cross in our hands than a gun."[9] They should lay down their lives, dying, not killing, in the name of Christ. As they put it, it is "hard to imagine Jesus enrolling for the concealed weapons class at Liberty University or anywhere else. And it is even harder to imagine Jesus approving of the words of Falwell as he openly threatened Muslims."[10]

In contrast, P. Andrew Sandlin—founder and president of the Center for Cultural Leadership—argues that justice is at the heart of God's kingdom and that justice can include the lethal defense of innocent life.[11] In "Pistol Packin' Jesus: A Response to Shane Claiborne," Sandlin claims that Jesus "would have supported—and does support—carrying firearms to defend that life." He regards Falwell's words as a "thoroughly *Christian* assertion." Sandlin maintains that Jesus would have carried a cross and a gun (if there had been guns at the time). He appeals to Luke 22:36, a text where Jesus tells the disciples to sell their cloaks to buy a sword. Sandlin understands Jesus's commands as instruction for self-defense.[12] Sandlin goes on to say that Jesus told Peter to put his sword away because of his unique redemptive mission. He had to go to the cross, not defend his innocent life. Sandlin appeals to some Old Testament passages that many claim offer support for killing in self-defense (Exod. 22:2-3; Ps. 82:4; and Prov. 24:10-12). He also notes the non-pacifist Jesus in Revelation 19:11-16, where Jesus "judges and makes war," "is clothed in a robe dipped in blood," and has coming from his mouth "a sharp sword with which to strike down the nations." According to Sandlin, Jesus would support the Second Amendment, and "he would be quite happy for his disciples to carry firearms" in order to protect innocent life. Sandlin concludes that both love and justice require the defense of innocent life, even if that means one must kill to defend that life.

Many of the passages of Scripture Sandlin references have been examined in previous chapters. I argue there that Jesus would not carry a gun. Revelation 19:11-16, however, seems to be a favorite of many Christian gun-rights advocates. Perhaps this is because it undeniably offers a *Braveheart*-like picture of Jesus, at least on the surface:

> Then I saw heaven opened, and there was a white horse! Its rider is called Faithful and True, and in righteousness he judges and makes war. His eyes are like a flame of fire, and on his head are many diadems; and he has a name inscribed that no one knows but himself. He is clothed in a robe dipped in blood, and his name is called The Word of God. And the armies of heaven, wearing fine linen, white and pure, were following him on white

horses. From his mouth comes a sharp sword with which to strike down the nations, and he will rule them with a rod of iron; he will tread the wine press of the fury of the wrath of God the Almighty. On his robe and on his thigh he has a name inscribed, "King of kings and Lord of lords."

The Jesus described here seems to resemble Christoph Waltz's Jesus in the Saturday Night Live spoof "Djesus Uncrossed," a video short in which Christ mows down his enemies with an automatic weapon. Grudem claims "John saw nothing morally offensive about portraying the activities of the risen Christ in martial terms."[13] Is such an interpretation fair to the text? Is the Jesus of Revelation 19 little more than a divine William Wallace hacking his enemies to pieces?

A closer look at the text in immediate and broader contexts illuminates its aim. This is a *metaphor*. As in the Old Testament prophets, the biblical writers use the warrior as a metaphor "to describe God's judgment in the end times."[14] When reading of a "robe dipped in blood," many easily jump to the conclusion that this is "a mark of the divine warrior splattered with the blood of enemies whom he has killed."[15] But this is a mistake. In this passage, the rider's robe is dipped in blood prior to the battle. The blood is his own, the blood of the Lamb who was slain. The sword coming from his mouth is not a physical sword. It is the word of God, through which God executes his judgment on the nations. And it is clear from the passage that God inexorably judges the wicked. But the slain Lamb of God is the center of worship and praise. He does not reign through violence. He is the Savior who conquers through suffering.

He also conquers through the truth of his word. At the culmination of all things, as God's kingdom comes and his will is done, the truth of God's word yields victory. Romano Guardini, Catholic priest and professor at the University of Berlin, gives a beautiful description of what will happen:

> Truth and power will become inseparable. . . . Stupendous event—
> fulfillment of all spiritual longing! The immeasurable truth of
> God: immeasurable power, the holy truth of God: holy, destruc-

tive, revolutionary, reconstructive power that will dominate all things! How will this come about? Through the word of Christ. Through his word spoken in history's last hour and valid for all eternity. . . . Dreadful hour for its enemies! Everything in us that shrinks from the light will have to go, for there will be no more shade . . . all existence will brim with truth and light.[16]

The sword of the rider on the white horse in Revelation 19 is the word of God. It is not an actual sword, and it in no way justifies the use of a gun against another human being.

Two very different pictures of Jesus are given by Claiborne and Sandlin. The weight of the evidence is on Claiborne's side. It seems clear that Jesus would not carry a gun. He told his disciples to put their swords away. He taught that those who live by the sword will die by the sword. His kingdom is not of this world, and therefore is not built upon violence. As far as we can know, he never personally carried a sword. Jesus's example is one of faith, hope, love, compassion, mercy, humility, and peace. This doesn't necessarily mean that his followers should never have or use a gun, but it does mean they should be peace builders. It at least means that a follower of Jesus should use violence only as a truly last resort, in the most extreme of circumstances. It also means that even in such cases, there may be times in which nonviolent resistance and even accepting one's own death are the right course of action. This is the example he gave for those who would imitate him: "But if you endure when you do right and suffer for it, you have God's approval. For to this you have been called, because Christ also suffered for you, leaving you an example, so that you should follow in his steps" (1 Pet. 2:20b–21).

The Impact of Guns on Character

How do guns shape us? What is their impact on our hearts, minds, and souls? Do they have any impact on our character?

Oliver Winchester thought they did. He praised the moral effect that the Model 73 repeater rifle (a semiautomatic firearm) had on the man who carried it: "for if there is anything that will make a

party of men, or one single man, stand up and fight to the last moment, it is the knowledge that he has a gun in his hands that will
not fail to do its duty."[17] The Model 73 was thought to be a source
of courage. It was at least advertised as such.

In chapter 1, we discussed Gun Culture 2.0. The main focus of
Gun Culture 2.0 is armed citizenship. To the extent that Gun Culture 2.0 instills in people a willingness to kill, it can be harmful
to their character.[18] My claim is not that owning and using a gun
necessarily compromise character. But if one does so, and adopts
much of what Gun Culture 2.0 involves, then owning and using a
gun can have a negative impact on one's character. Here's why.

Most human beings have "a deep-seated psychological resistance
to killing."[19] This is obviously a good feature of human psychology. This resistance is grounded in human empathy that recognizes
others, including our enemies, as fellow human beings. How we
think about, value, and use guns can affect the way we view and
treat others.

Killing becomes easier when the enemy is dehumanized.[20] In
military contexts, this can be accomplished by conditioning a person to fire a gun at another human being without really thinking
about the action being performed. In the military, this could occur by training soldiers to fire at human-like targets and rewarding
or punishing them based on their success in such exercises. The
hoped-for result is that soldiers will develop quick-shoot reflexes,
not thinking about the fact that they are killing another human
being at the moment of the conditioned response. This is a sad
necessity and reality of war. Many later feel revulsion at what they
have done or struggle with it in other ways.

As noted above, firing at human-shaped targets is a significant
part of Gun Culture 2.0. For example, in one account of a rolling
thunder shotgun drill, a line of shooters stands ten yards away from
steel plates shaped like human silhouettes. The point is to practice
reloads and manipulations so that the shooter is prepared for a
home invasion. To do this, the first shooter at the left end of the line
waits for a timer. When it goes off, he rapidly loads a shell and fires.
After he fires, the next shooter does the same, and so on down the
line. Then, the first shooter tube-loads a shell and emergency-loads

another, firing twice. The next round, each shooter tube-feeds two shells, emergency-reloads one, and fires three. Next, each tube-feeds three shells, emergency-reloads one, and fires four. In this exercise, rewards and punishments are given, depending on how successful each individual shooter is:

> Rolling Thunder is a great way to hone your shotgun skills. It adds a unique stress because not only are you competing against yourself, you're working as a team to move as quickly and accurately as possible. If even one shooter fumbles his reloads and/or botches his shots the entire line suffers as the final time for the drill rises. Bonus points if you hone your dual, triple, or quad loads during the drill.[21]

Another example of a rolling thunder drill involves a line of shooters with handguns, about ten yards or so from paper human silhouette targets at night. A person with a flashlight shines a light on the first target, and immediately the first shooter fires. This is repeated down the line. These types of competitions and other forms of shooting practice involve creating a quick-shot reflex, which can undermine the natural resistance to killing another human being.

There are justifications for such training that should not be dismissed out of hand. Good defensive-firearms training enables a person to master the different components of skillful shooting, which reduces the cognitive load one experiences in a crisis situation. The result could be that "not having to worry as much about the physical details of gunhandling and marksmanship frees the mind to make good, ethical decisions about the use of force in self-defense."[22] The desired outcome is less purely reflexive decision making when a threat is present.

Granting the above, it is nevertheless a real possibility that repetitive training with human-like targets can harm character. Such harm may or may not occur, in any individual case. But it is a live possibility, one we must be aware of. On balance, we must decide, in Spirit-led wisdom, whether these possible costs outweigh the likely benefits.

The resistance to killing can also be thwarted when we are encouraged to see our enemies—be they military enemies or other members of our own society—as *morally inferior*. This can be done through racist epithets, as was the case in Vietnam and Iraq. It can also be done by seeing the enemy as evil, as morally inferior and deserving of death. Recall that some in the gun-rights movement refer to criminals as "wolves" and themselves as "sheepdogs" protecting the "sheep." The wolves are the bad guys, the sheepdogs are the good guys protecting the innocent but defenseless sheep. The idea is not merely that criminals are less moral than others. It is that they are less valuable, even though they are fellow human beings.

But how, in particular, can this harm character? If our resistance to killing others is weakened by conditioning or by seeing them as morally inferior, empathy for them is weakened. But many psychological studies show that empathy is connected to altruistic acts and to acts involving helping others. It also plays a role in preventing aggression and violence. Empathy is important for good character. Weakening empathy by dehumanizing others in these ways harms our character. It makes it more difficult to have virtues that are deeply connected with empathy. Compassion, sympathy, and kindness come to mind. If we see others as less than human, this can lead to moral vices, including callousness, cruelty, and malice.

Does this mean that killing another in self-defense or war is never justified, on the basis of concerns about character? No. Nor does it mean that soldiers or others who engage in these actions have bad character. Such an act may be morally justified, but it is nevertheless tragic. The morally virtuous person who as a last resort kills an assailant in self-defense (or in defense of another person) may not be guilty of sin per se. Nevertheless, if that person has good character, is empathetic, compassionate, and loving, he "will feel regret at having been the agent of killing."[23] The loss of life, even if necessary to protect other life, will be a source of pain and regret.

Sadly, such callousness and lack of empathy are present among some Christian gun enthusiasts. As one observer put it after the San Bernardino shooting:

I see Christian friends on social media post about how excited they are to buy a new gun and boast about their stopping power. . . . Much of this comes down to tone, tenor and attitude. Whether a Christian owns a gun to protect their family is their own decision. But the way they approach that gun and speak about it can be chilling. Even though I think people have the right to a gun if they prove themselves trustworthy, I still get chills when I see Facebook friends post ads about their weapon's power, or proudly talk how they just bought a new handgun—and look how awesome it is! These are Christians, people who identify as being pro-life, bragging about their weapon's ability to kill, and often filled with macho bluster that seems to say "Jesus says love your enemy, but I'm ready to blow them away if I have to." It's dismaying—if you must own a gun, especially as a Christian, own one soberly and with regret that this world has brought you to this point. But Christian, never boast about a weapon that can kill, that is designed expressly for taking life, and that can do so effectively. Never be happy or proud to own an instrument of death. That power is a sober, sorrowful one to wield.[24]

Has the culture of some segments of the Christian church in America taken on non-Christian aspects of Gun Culture 2.0? Clearly it has. The ability of Christians to kill speaks to character.

Courage and Guns

Clearly, there are ways in which guns can hinder our pursuit of empathy, of virtues like compassion and kindness. We've seen that guns can become idols. We've discussed the conflict that can arise when we seek to love others but also seek to protect them from those who would harm them. But what about courage? Surely facing down an intruder or assailant with a gun is a courageous act.

Sometimes, using a gun is an act of cowardice rather than of courage. When people act from fear and cowardice and have the power of a gun at their disposal, it is a recipe for tragedy. This was the case in the shooting death of Lucy McBath's son, Jordan Davis. The shooter felt threatened because Jordan and three other unarmed African American boys were playing their music too loud and wouldn't turn it down. This is an act not only of irrational fear but also of lethal cowardice.[25]

The coward lets fear dictate his attitudes and actions. The courageous person is not controlled by fear. She does not give in to it. But what else comes to mind when you think of a courageous person? In American culture, the image of the heroic warrior dominates. Movies serve up an endless array of action heroes, soldiers, and cowboys who face up to adversity, danger, and death. This shapes our understanding of courage. But is Christian courage something more or something different? What is Christlike courage, and what does it tell us about Christians and guns?[26]

Christian courage, at its root, is grounded in love, not in human power. Both the heroic warrior and the martyr are willing "to risk death for the sake of something they love."[27] Courage can help us resist and overcome our fears, leading to a more fulfilled life. It not only can help us to do what is right and to be good but can also help us to more clearly see what is right and good. Fear, by contrast, if left unchecked, can cloud our judgments and inhibit us from doing and being all that we ought. The aggressive courage of movie heroes like John McClane, Rocky, or John Wayne has a time and place. But for the Christian, it is the courage of the martyr that is the best example of Christian courage. That is the kind of courage that Jesus has.

The courage of the action hero is valuable; it is good. To risk one's own life, to fight against evil for the sake of justice, is admirable. The courageous action hero uses his strength, often physical or military power, to defeat evil and save the innocent. But there is a danger here. This kind of courage can lead us to put our faith in our own powers and abilities. In some cases, it can lead us to place our confidence in the powers and abilities of our weapons.

The courage of the martyr is different. This is a courage in which one suffers and endures an evil that either cannot or should not be defeated by physical force. It is radical. It reveals a unique kind of strength. It reveals a love that is greater than fear of death. It reveals a truly self-giving form of love, in the mold of Jesus himself. If martyrdom is the paradigm of courage, this shows us "that this virtue can find expression as much or more in suffering and weakness as it can in striking out against a threat."[28] Not only is this true, but when we make martyrdom our paradigm of courage, it "enables *anyone willing to endure suffering for the sake of love* to echo this supreme example of courage in their own lives, and leaves physical power, with its attendant gender, health, and age limitations, out of the picture."[29]

What does this tell us about guns and our willingness to use them? It tells us that the greatest form of courage is to offer up one's life, to refrain from killing another in self-defense. This doesn't necessarily mean that self-defense is always or even usually wrong. As we've seen, a case can be made that it is sometimes justified. But it does mean that the courage of Christ is most clearly on display when we sacrifice our lives for the good, including the good of those who would take our lives from us.

Imagine a person who is convinced that she should not kill others in self-defense. When her conviction is put to the test, when she is asked to endure suffering and even death, "physical strength, brute force, better weapons, and human power are not what make [her] strong. These things have been . . . laid aside. To endure the danger that threatens and her own fear, [she] needs strength of soul—and that is the heart of courage."[30]

Love, not a gun, can make such courage, such self-sacrifice, possible.

Conclusion

After the Columbine shooting, the editors of *Christianity Today* offered the following observations:

> Jesus said, Do not be afraid of those who kill the body (Luke 12:4-5). Angels often declared, "Fear not!"—even in very dangerous settings. We know that our fate is in God's hands, not our

firepower. And we know that human life is so valuable that God sent his Son to die for us. That means, whatever is designed to take life must be treated with the utmost seriousness and caution. We may not know all of what Jesus would do about guns and our violent society, but we know more than enough to speak out against the idolatry of lethal power.[31]

There are strong reasons for thinking that Jesus wouldn't carry a gun. Why, then, do so many of his followers insist that Jesus would support the Second Amendment? Why do they appear to revel in the power of their guns? Why do they seem quick to justify and even love violence? Christians will disagree about many things related to guns and public policy. However, one thing we should all agree on is that the use of a gun against another human being made in God's image is not to be celebrated. The death of any person is tragic. Our attitudes toward guns in particular, and violence in general, should reflect this truth.

But it's not just the *celebration* of using guns against others that we must avoid. We should be much less apt to *tolerate* the use of guns against others. An uncritical embrace of American gun culture is inconsistent with beliefs about the sanctity of life. We must be careful that we are not eager to kill, nor to take killing another human being—any other human being—too lightly. All human beings, no matter how good or bad, have equal inherent value because they are made in the image of God. We must be sure we realize what it means to kill another person.

We must be vigilant about who we are and who we are becoming. For those who own and use guns, this includes not being conformed to the evil aspects of Gun Culture 2.0 but instead being transformed by the renewing of our minds (see Rom. 12:1-2). This renewal happens as we adapt to the culture of the gospel rather than the culture of the gun. To the extent that carrying and using a gun harms our character and does not reflect the character of Jesus, we have good reasons not to do so.

We need to examine our attitudes about guns. Are we trusting in guns for things that we should be relying on God to grant us? As Christians, faith means much more than just trusting God to forgive us. Faith means trusting God with *everything*. This includes our possessions, our lives, and the lives of those we love. We may choose to own a gun, but we must never trust in a gun rather than God. If we do, our faith is deeply flawed. To be blunt, we must repent of such idolatry. False idols make us feel powerful, but God is ultimately in control. Only God offers ultimate security. Only God will never fail us.

7

MORE THAN THOUGHTS AND PRAYERS

On October 1, 2015, a man with a gun murdered nine students and one professor at Umpqua Community College near Roseburg, Oregon. After a shootout with police, he took his own life. As was and still is the norm, politicians—including John Kasich, Lindsey Graham, and Joe Biden—expressed their "thoughts and prayers" on behalf of the victims, their families, and their communities. President Barack Obama, however, said, "Our thoughts and prayers are not enough."[1] He was right.

Other politicians and activists have echoed President Obama's sentiment. After the church shooting in Sutherland Springs, Texas, Shannon Watts, the founder of Moms Demand Action for Gun Sense in America, proclaimed, "If thoughts and prayers alone prevented gun violence, we wouldn't be shot in places of worship. God calls on us to ACT." Georgia congressman John Lewis, in a similar vein, urged, "We must do more than mourn and pray for those murdered in Texas. We must act." And Senator Richard Blumenthal tweeted, "Prayers are important but insufficient. After another unspeakable tragedy, Congress must act—or be complicit."[2]

Providing comfort and compassion through expressions of sympathy and prayer are important parts of any Christian response to gun violence. In James 5, we're told that the prayer of a righteous person is "powerful and effective." But prayer on its own is simply not enough. Consider the words from James 2:15-17:

If a brother or sister is naked and lacks daily food, and one of you says to them, "Go in peace; keep warm and eat your fill," and yet you do not supply their bodily needs, what is the good of that? So faith by itself, if it has no works, is dead.

Consider also the many potential victims of gun violence who live in fear of an abusive spouse or parent who has a gun in the house. Consider schoolchildren, worshipers, moviegoers, concert-goers, college students, all of whom live in the knowledge that they could be next. Think of first responders who come under fire simply because they are trying to protect or treat people in their communities. Is the Christian answer to this really nothing more than thoughts, prayers, and placing our hope in "a good guy with a gun"? Certainly not.

It's not just the easy acquisition of guns and concealed-carry permits that are problematic. It's also that one doesn't need to demonstrate proficiency with a gun in order to purchase one. Consider Kentucky, a state where guns are a significant part of many people's lives. During 2012–2017, at least thirty-six children in Kentucky accidentally shot either themselves or another child.[3] The average age of victim and shooter was nine. These shootings caused fifteen deaths.

Among them, a five-year-old boy accidentally killed his two-year-old sister with "My First Rifle." In another case, a three-year-old boy shot his fifteen-month-old sister in the face, and upon doing so immediately started screaming, "I'm sorry, Mom!" His father reported that he never secured his gun but left it in an unlocked case. On this day, the case was on top of a pile of clothes on the closet floor. In yet another instance, a grandfather was cleaning his .38 revolver in a room with his grandchildren. He put it on the coffee table and went to another room to get something. His four-year-old grandson picked up the gun and accidentally shot his six-year-old sister in the face. She did not survive. In none of these cases were any criminal charges filed. Some argue that parents and other adults who are responsible for leaving unsecured weapons where children can access them should be held legally responsible. Sometimes children and other innocent people die, not because of a bad guy with a gun or the absence of a good guy with a gun, but because someone is careless with a gun. This should be taken into account as we consider what possible changes we might make in gun policy.

What, then, can be done about gun violence in America? No law will be foolproof. But this doesn't mean that laws can't make a significant difference. If we have good reason to believe that some laws can reduce gun violence, then we should put them in place.

What other steps can be taken to reduce gun violence? The mere presence of guns does not explain the level of violent crime in America. Canada and France have high levels of gun ownership but relatively low levels of homicide compared to the United States.[4] But the fact that gun ownership is not the sole explanation does not mean that it is not part of the explanation. We need to figure out what else is contributing to the violence and address that as well. We should work to reduce gun violence in America.

Data

We have less data on guns and gun violence in America than we should, in large measure due to the Dickey Amendment.[5] This legislation, passed in 1996 with support from the NRA, prohibited the Centers for Disease Control and Prevention (CDC) from allocating money to anything that would promote gun control. Gun research could still be carried out using federal funds, but the amendment led to a 96 percent decrease in CDC funding for gun research from 1996 to 2013, when the freeze on funding was lifted. In recent years, gun research is on the rise thanks to funding from universities and the private sector.

Even with this increase, it can be difficult to draw clearly supported general conclusions based on data.[6] Some have performed studies that they say support several claims, including that (1) guns are a very important and effective means of self-defense; (2) stricter gun-control laws will prevent law-abiding citizens from having guns and using them for self-defense; and (3) stricter gun laws will encourage criminals to have and use lethal weapons. On the other side, people argue that studies show that a high rate of private gun ownership causes a higher rate of homicides. They offer data that show that a gun in the home is correlated with a higher rate of suicide in the home, especially young people (under nineteen years of age). The easy availability of guns in general leads to more (and more successful) suicide attempts.

The disagreement can be summed up in this way. A few individual researchers, such as Gary Kleck and John Lott, argue that private ownership of guns is very beneficial. Others—primarily medical researchers and public health scholars, and a few philosophers—argue that these alleged benefits are overstated. In fact, they argue, the costs are very high. Finally, a 2004 report by a National Research Council Committee found that claims about millions of self-defense uses of guns occurring each year are unfounded. It also rejected claims that shall-issue carry permits are highly beneficial.[7] It found that "the research on the connections between guns and homicide, violent crimes in general, suicide, and accidents are [sic] less than convincing."[8] This applies to both pro-gun and pro-control research.

Given this, what should we do? It would take at least another entire book to examine the relevant studies, and their strengths and weaknesses, in sufficient detail. As a starting point, I would suggest Philip J. Cook and Kristin A. Goss, *The Gun Debate: What Everyone Needs to Know*, for a fair and unbiased summary of many of these issues.[9] More research has been done since 2004 that supports stricter gun laws. It will be helpful to look at some of the research on both sides of the debate. Doing so will reveal how statistics can often be misused and evidence misconstrued. This is the case for advocates of both gun rights and gun control.

The Case of Chicago

Consider the city of Chicago.[10] Chicago has strict gun laws. Yet it also has a very high level of gun violence. Many advocates of the status quo point to this as evidence that restrictive gun laws don't work. It's easy to see why. But it's a mistake to draw this conclusion.

It is easy to go outside of the city of Chicago or to another state to buy guns. They are then brought into the city for use or sale. In fact, from 2008 to 2012, 1,375 guns that had been used in criminal activities were confiscated by the Chicago police. The source of nearly 20 percent of these guns was one store located a few miles outside the city limits. It doesn't take much effort to see that strict laws in a city won't work in such a situation.

In fact, what the case of Chicago arguably shows is that we need stricter laws to be more widespread if they are to be effective. To remove the sources that provide easy access to guns to those who should not have them, more widespread laws are needed.

Even some smaller-scale approaches have been effective. For example, in Milwaukee a majority of the guns used in crimes that were recovered within a year of their first retail sale were traced to one gun dealer.[11] In response to negative publicity about this, the dealer in question made some changes. For example, the dealer no longer sold "junk guns." These guns are both cheap and low in quality but can be sold for a very high profit on the street. As a result, there was a 76 percent reduction in the flow of guns from this store to criminals, as well as a 44 percent reduction in new gun crimes in Milwaukee.

The Brady Act

In 1981, during an unsuccessful attempt to assassinate President Ronald Reagan, his press secretary, James Brady, was shot. Both he and his wife, Sarah, became leaders in the gun-control movement and were instrumental in the passing of the Brady Handgun Violence Prevention Act of 1994. The act required federally licensed gun dealers to do a background check on individuals seeking to buy a handgun. It also implemented a five-day waiting period before a customer could take possession of a gun. In 2000, President Bill Clinton proclaimed that the Brady Act was a success, preventing many criminals from buying handguns, thereby saving many lives.

But is this correct?[12] Was the Brady Act a success, as Clinton claimed? In its first five years, 312,000 applications for purchasing a gun from a licensed dealer were denied because the applicant had a felony record or was disqualified for some other reason. Some drew the same conclusion that President Clinton did. Guns are more lethal than knives and other weapons. Given this, fewer guns in the wrong hands would mean fewer homicides.

A study of the Brady Act's effectiveness, however, found that it had essentially no effect on the overall homicide and suicide rates. At best, it may have had a small positive impact. The authors of the study are quick to point out, however, that a different regulatory approach could be more effective. Some have argued that the Brady Act was too narrow. They point to the fact while those convicted of a misdemeanor assault on an intimate partner were prohibited from buying a gun, persons convicted of other forms of misdemeanor assaults were not. Neither were those who abused alcohol, which is positively correlated with committing acts of violence.[13]

The Gun Crowd's Guru

There is continuing controversy over the research done by John Lott, whom *Newsweek* magazine once called "the Gun Crowd's Guru." Lott is one of a small minority of researchers who are strong gun-rights advocates. In short, Lott argues that more guns lead to less crime. Lott admits that many factors influence crime rates, but he also argues that nondiscretionary handgun laws are important. Nondiscretionary, or shall-issue laws, dictate that the state must respect the right of individuals to own and carry a concealed weapon unless there is a demonstrable reason to deny this right (e.g., certain types of criminal records or a history of significant mental illness). According to Lott, such laws are the most cost-effective method for reducing crime. They deter crime, especially violent crime, including murder, rape, robbery, and aggravated assault. He also concludes that there is no statistically significant increase in accidental shootings due to such laws.[14]

Many challenge Lott's conclusions, as well as how he arrives at them.[15] Hugh LaFollette examines Lott's case for concluding that shall-issue laws dramatically reduce violent crime but do not cause a significant increase in accidental shootings.[16] The use of statistics to support policy positions, especially when it involves complex manipulation of the statistics, is worrying to many, including many statisticians. This is a problem for Lott and other pro-gun researchers, as well as for those who are pro-control.

Two significant factors make figuring out the cause-and-effect relationship between gun laws and violent crime very difficult. First, those things that impact violent crime rates in a state change from year to year. Crime often comes in waves, and this makes it difficult to decipher the role of right-to-carry laws. Second, the other factors that impact crime can play a different role across counties, states, or nations. Poverty may be less significant where a stronger social safety net exists, for example.

Researchers who favor stricter gun laws point out many flaws in Lott's methods, and Lott offers defenses to many of these charges. At times, though, his replies are flawed. For example, when his assumptions are questioned, LaFollette argues, Lott is guilty of "tinkering with those assumptions and trotting out even more complex statistical jargon."[17] LaFollette admits that Lott's methods and conclusions might be valid, but considering many of these and other criticisms, there is good reason to doubt it. He concludes with the following criticism of Lott's work:

> He does not seem to see, and therefore, could not possibly accept, one inference from his findings. He claims that "for every 1,000 additional people with permits, there are 0.3 fewer murders, 2.4 fewer rapes, 21 fewer robberies, and 14.1 fewer aggravated assaults." He also claims that the benefits of shall-issue laws are cumulative and linear: the more permits we issue . . . the greater the benefits. If we accept his findings and this explicit assumption, then more than two-thirds of all states would not have a single homicide. If we issued 1.2 million permits throughout the combined six northeastern states, then there would not be a single homicide in that area of the country—although that region has nearly 18% of the US population. These claims are implausible.[18]

These claims are indeed implausible. LaFollette concludes that while more data and better studies are needed, we do have reasons to think that stricter gun laws can reduce homicides, suicides, and the fear of gun violence that exists in America. Moreover, Lott's proposed solution to crime ignores the other causes, such as the drug trade, poor education systems, and poverty. It is, at best, a stopgap solution to these deeper problems. Consider where this might lead:

> A highly armed society like ours is bound to be dangerous—and in a dangerous society, where rule of law is increasingly eroded and deadly violence more likely, a gun is increasingly the only thing providing a chance of personal security. But who wants to live in that world? And why must we think such a world is inevitable? . . . In our American democracy, we have higher ambitions.[19]

Such a world is not inevitable. We can take concrete steps to reduce gun violence. We can take steps to realize our high American ambitions of peace and security that do not rest on widespread gun ownership, concealed carry, and gun use, similar to "the electric détente when two warring gangs hold each other off with pointed weapons."[20]

There is good evidence that stricter gun laws should be part of the overall approach to reducing gun violence.[21] The rate of gun murders in the United States, 3.2 per 100,000 people, places it twenty-sixth in the world. Countries like Honduras (68.4), Colombia (27.1), and Mexico (10.0) are ahead of us. But when we compare particular cities, the comparison is not so favorable. New Orleans has a rate of 62.1 gun murders per 100,000 people, Miami 23.7, and Phoenix 10.6. More revealing is the fact that the United States has a higher overall homicide rate than other developed nations with stricter gun laws, including the United Kingdom, France, Germany, Spain, and Japan.

Within our borders, evidence shows that in states with more gun laws, there are fewer homicides and suicides. As one study found, "In states that have the most [gun] laws, there is a 42 percent reduction in fatalities, compared to those states with the least number of laws. You can't necessarily say one absolutely led to the other . . . but you can say those things are related."[22]

To draw stronger conclusions here, we need more data. It is difficult to demonstrate cause-and-effect relationships in such studies, with wide scope, for many reasons. In the case of gun violence, a variety of factors contributes to the problem. Nevertheless, there is a growing body of evidence supporting stricter laws as one part of a multipronged approach to reducing gun violence. We ignore it at our peril.

A Proposal for Legal Action

When someone mentions creating stricter gun laws, one often hears something like "Prohibition didn't work with alcohol, and it won't work with guns!" Often, when people call for more regulations, the assumption is that they are opposed to the Second Amendment or want a complete ban on all firearms. That's not my position. In fact, my position is supported by the history of Prohibition in America.[23] Prohibition banned the sale and transportation of alcohol. When Prohibition was repealed, state laws governing the sale, consumption, and transportation of alcohol were not eliminated. There are restrictions on who can purchase alcohol, what types of alcohol can be purchased, where it can be purchased, and where it can be consumed. The proposals here are similar. They do not constitute a ban on guns but, rather, reasonable controls on their purchase and use designed to limit harm.

As we've seen, there is no easy, one-size-fits-all fix to gun violence in America. But the steps below are worth considering and implementing as a significant part of the solution. Again, I am not calling for a repeal of the Second Amendment. This must be kept in mind. My position is that there are many things we can and should do that are supported by research and experts from many fields, including law, medicine, public health, public safety, philosophy, and theology. The following suggestions are not meant to be all-inclusive and are drawn from a variety of sources. There may be other effective strategies for reducing gun violence. But this is a good place to start.

Universal Background Checks

A system should be implemented requiring background checks for any person who purchases a firearm, without exception. All sales, including multiple sales of the same gun, should be facilitated through a federally licensed dealer. It would also be helpful to increase the maximum time allowed for the FBI to complete such checks to ten days. For such a system to be effective, sufficient resources should be given to the ATF (Bureau of Alcohol, Tobacco, Firearms and Explosives), so that it can properly oversee federally licensed gun dealers. Gun dealers should be subject to tort liability, that is, to paying damages to victims of gun violence when their negligence has led to such harm. To do this, the Protection of Lawful Commerce in Arms Act should be repealed. Dealers who make unlawful sales, or violate the law in other ways, should receive adequate penalties.[24]

Expand the Conditions for Who Can Purchase a Firearm

The goal here is to deter people who are at high risk of committing acts of violence with a gun from obtaining one. Persons who have been convicted of a violent misdemeanor should be prohibited from purchasing a firearm for fifteen years. Those convicted of committing a violent crime as a juvenile should not be allowed to purchase a gun until they are thirty. Anyone convicted of two or more drug- or alcohol-related crimes in a three-year period should not be allowed to purchase a gun for ten years. All the following persons should be banned from purchasing a gun: anyone convicted of any drug-trafficking crime, anyone under twenty-one years of age, anyone who has violated any type of restraining order that was issued due to a threat of violence, anyone who is under a temporary restraining order for violence or the threat of violence, and anyone convicted of misdemeanor stalking. In addition, those who have a serious mental illness that poses a threat to themselves or others should not be allowed to purchase a gun.[25]

A Federal Red Flag Law

The state of Maryland is one of many states that has implemented a "red flag" gun safety law.[26] It initially appears to be very effective. This law allows persons, such as police officers, family members, or health-care professionals, to make a legal request that firearms be temporarily removed from potentially dangerous individuals by the courts. In roughly half of the cases, a final order was issued. This means that the guns are not immediately returned to their owners, who may be banned from purchasing or owning a gun for one year. In cases where a mental health problem is involved, and the individual receives treatment or medication, the guns are returned. According to Montgomery County sheriff Darren Popkin, "These orders are not only being issued appropriately; they are saving lives." Five of the first 302 requests under the new law involved possible school shootings. A federal firearm restraining order system similar to Maryland's can and should be created.

Repeal Stand-Your-Ground Laws

We saw in chapter 2 that stand-your-ground laws are susceptible to and in part born out of racial (and other forms of) prejudice, and that many who rely on them are not using firearms as a last resort. There are several other problems with such laws.[27] Private citizens are given powers that have normally been reserved for police officers, but they are not given the requisite training. A former Miami chief of police puts it this way: "Trying to control shootings by members of a well-trained and disciplined police department is a daunting enough task. Laws like 'stand your ground' give citizens unfettered power and discretion with no accountability. It is a recipe for disaster."[28]

Recent studies show that stand-your-ground laws increase homicide rates. They do not reduce assaults, robberies, or rapes. Defendants who initiate fights or shoot unarmed people, sometimes pursuing them, are claiming that they are simply standing their ground. This is unacceptable.[29] In sum, "stand-your-ground laws encourage the use of deadly force. These laws open the door to a more dangerous world where everyone feels pressure to carry a gun—and if he feels threatened, shoot first and tell his story later."[30] For these and other reasons, such laws should be repealed.

A Mandatory Federal Gun Safety Course

To purchase or possess a firearm, all persons should be required to pass a sufficiently demanding and detailed gun safety course.[31] We require drivers to demonstrate competence in driving cars before we license them to do so. The same requirement should be implemented for gun purchasers and owners. A skills, storage, and general safety test should be created. The license should be renewable, so that gun owners must demonstrate their competency on a regular basis, as automobile drivers do. The justification is the same in both cases. More competent drivers and more competent gun owners mean fewer injuries and deaths.

Technological Solutions

One easy solution, aimed at preventing easy access to guns in the home, is the gun safe. But if one wants quick access to a gun in a self-defense scenario in the home, opening the safe may take too long. There are emerging technologies for smart guns, which employ biometric technology or an RFID (radio-frequency identification) "key" that unlocks the gun, enabling it to fire. This has an added advantage. Stolen guns with this type of technology could not be fired. In addition, gun accidents would decrease and suicidal teens wouldn't be able to use their parents' guns to kill themselves.[32]

The Bison Fingerprint Trigger Lock looks promising. The trigger lock falls immediately after the owner places his finger on the lock. The ease and speed at which this lock works mean that it can be used quickly in self-defense, and the lock also prevents people other than the owner from firing the gun.

Finally, resources should be devoted to the development of highly effective but nonlethal weapons for self-defense. If such weapons could be developed, the need—whether merely felt or actual—for guns to use in self-defense would be eradicated.

Assault Weapons and High-Capacity Magazines

A careful and applicable definition of what counts as an assault weapon should be created. Then a ban on the sale of such weapons should be implemented. In addition, the sale and possession of high-capacity magazines, defined as anything over ten rounds, should be banned.[33]

Liability Insurance for Gun Owners and Users

Another strategy for reducing harm done by gun violence is to require gun liability insurance.[34] We require insurance for automobile drivers. When a driver harms someone else, the driver's insurance company pays the victim. If you don't have a car, or don't drive a car, then you don't pay for insurance. If you are a cause of harm, then you are morally and legally responsible to compensate those who have been harmed.

Similarly, gun users and gun owners would need to purchase gun liability insurance, to compensate the victims of gun violence. Those with multiple guns would need to pay higher premiums, just as those with multiple cars do. Those who demonstrate greater competence, through taking gun safety courses, for example, would see reduced premiums.

Gun liability insurance would compensate people harmed by guns. It would financially protect gun owners who are responsible for such harm. It would also motivate people to be careful with the firearms they own. Not all gun owners would be more responsible, just as not all drivers are more responsible due to the insurance system. But many would. And this is not merely a policy that gun-control advocates desire. The NRA affirms that purchasing gun liability insurance is a good idea.

Guns and the risk of harm are inseparable. It is only fair that those who choose to own or use guns bear the financial cost of that harm.

Funding for Research on Gun Violence

The federal government should provide significant funds for more research on guns and gun violence. It should focus on the causes of such violence as well as on what solutions might be implemented to reduce it. These funds would be directed to the Centers for Disease Control and Prevention, the National Institutes of Health, and the National Institute of Justice. Perhaps incentives could also be put in place to encourage more private and university funding of such research.[35]

Protect Everyone's Rights

These suggestions protect the rights of those who are competent to own and use firearms, allowing them to do so for hunting, recreation, or self-defense purposes. They would make it more likely that each individual gun owner will be responsible. They protect the right to life that is threatened and often violated by those who have no business owning a gun but nevertheless do. If implemented and enforced, these suggestions will reduce the level of gun violence in America.

Indeed, implementing the above proposals is one way to apply the wisdom of Proverbs 24:11-12:

> If you hold back from rescuing those taken away
>   to death,
>   those who go staggering to the slaughter;
> if you say, "Look, we did not know this"—
>   does not he who weighs the heart perceive it?
> Does not he who keeps watch over your soul know it?

If it is true that we can do more to save innocent lives from death by gun violence, then we must act. We must act to save the life of the suicidal teenager. We must act to save the life of the toddler whose dad carelessly leaves a loaded gun within her reach. We must save the life of the victim of domestic violence. We must save the lives of many at their school, church, mosque, synagogue, movie theater, concert, or office. No law will entirely eliminate gun violence. But these proposals, properly enforced, will save actual human lives. We know it, and we must do all we can to rescue those who would otherwise face death looking down the barrel of a gun.

A Proposal for Moral Action

We should offer our thoughts and prayers. Of course we should. But we should also do more. Much more.

The church can certainly provide support for the policy changes discussed above, seeking to educate, motivate, and inspire followers of Jesus to *do something* about gun violence.

The church can be a part of the solution to gun violence by being the church. The mission of the church is to preach and teach the gospel, and to live it out. The church should fight injustice, seek to transform communities, be a place where people are being changed and equipped to make a difference in the world.

Perhaps instead of arguing about gun control on social media, Christians might volunteer to be a Big Brother or Big Sister. Perhaps a church could adopt a school and provide tutoring and mentorship to children. Or perhaps all the churches in a city might band together and address the inequalities present in public education due to economic, racial, and social differences. The church should do all that it can to provide hope for all people, attacking some of the root causes of gun violence.

Make "Little Christs"

In his classic book *Mere Christianity*, C. S. Lewis writes that "Every Christian is to become a little Christ. The whole purpose of becoming a Christian is simply nothing else."[36] This happens, according to Lewis, as we come to let God have his way in us, as we come to share more and more in the life of Christ. This thought from Lewis also reflects Paul's desire for the Galatians, that "Christ is formed in you" (Gal. 4:19). In short, following Christ necessarily includes becoming like Christ.

The church in America has been too focused on getting people in the door rather than getting Christ into people. We must not only tell people to become more like Christ, but we must also teach them how to actually do it. We must offer, as Dallas Willard urges, a curriculum for Christlikeness.[37] We must be and make actual disciples of Jesus. We must seek to do what Jesus commanded and teach others how to do the same (Matt. 28:18-20). We need Sunday school classes focused on how we can learn to love our enemies. We need mentors who reflect the other-centered humility and love of Christ described in Philippians 2:1-11. And we need to learn how we can participate in the divine nature, how we can be persons of faith, goodness, knowledge, self-control, endurance, godliness, kindness, and love (2 Pet. 1:3-11).

In short, we need to seek to become "little Christs." We need to make loving God and others the primary focus of our lives. If we do this, many of the evils both in and outside of the church will be eradicated. If we do this, fewer people will suffer the harms caused by gun violence, because the hearts of people and the structures of our society will be more just and more loving.

Care for Our Sisters and Brothers

Jesus made it clear that love is central to following him: "By this everyone will know that you are my disciples, if you have love for one another" (John 13:35). Many American Christians point to self-defense and protecting their family to justify their opposition to stricter gun laws of any kind. This perspective is much too limited. Surely we must think of the welfare of others, too.

Bernard Howard, pastor of Good Shepherd Anglican Church in New York City, makes this point very well:

> One conceptual barrier to gun control that American Christians have cited is the importance of the availability of guns for protecting one's family. It's said that we have a duty to be

our "brother's keeper" (Genesis 4:9). But there's nothing in Scripture to suggest that keeping your brother means obtaining military-grade weaponry to protect him from every possible threat. What's more, the New Testament teaches that a Christian's ties to other believers are just as strong, if not stronger, than to family members (Mark 3:31–35). Keeping your brother must therefore include seeking the welfare of fellow Christians in the inner city areas where the threat of gun death is greatest. Maintaining permissive gun laws does nothing to protect those brothers and sisters. In any case, the measures being proposed by most gun control advocates would not prevent Americans from keeping firearms in their own home, where they could be used for self-defense.[38]

It's not just our brothers and sisters who live in dangerous areas that we must love; it's also those who live in dangerous homes. The church must do a better job protecting victims of domestic violence. Unfortunately, some churches simply do nothing about this. Examples are plentiful. One day Lucia came to see a minister of a church near her home. She shared that "I'm worried for my kids. . . . The problem is my husband. He beats me sometimes. Mostly he is a good man. But sometimes he becomes very angry and he hits me. . . . One time he broke my arm and I had to go to the hospital. . . . I went to my priest twenty years ago. I've been trying to follow his advice. The priest said I should rejoice in my sufferings because they bring me closer to Jesus. He said, 'Jesus suffered because he loved us.' He said, 'If you love Jesus, accept the beatings and bear them gladly, as Jesus bore the cross.'"[39] Apart from being a perversion of what it means that Christ suffered and died for us, this kind of "advice" leaves people in great danger, more so if a gun is in the home.

Many women have been told that it is their Christian duty to remain in the home even if their husband is violent. But this is not their duty. Their duty is to protect themselves and their children. But they need help to do so, and the church must provide such help. It can do so by providing or supporting emergency shelters for victims of domestic violence. It must do so by confronting the abusers in its midst and reporting them to law enforcement. It must do so by correcting bad theology that justifies abuse and teaches the abused to simply accept it.

As we've seen, a gun in the home can exacerbate domestic violence. Turning a blind eye to the dangers of guns, and to the fact of domestic violence among church members, does great harm. Doing nothing more to limit the availability of guns also does great harm. It must stop.

Build Good and Safe Communities

Just as we care for those who are brothers and sisters in Christ, we should also care for our brother and sister human beings. In a discussion of the sixth commandment—"You shall not murder"—John Calvin explains that

> since the Lord has bound the whole human race by a kind of unity, the safety of all ought to be considered as entrusted to each. In general, therefore, all violence and injustice, and every kind of harm from which our neighbor's body suffers, is prohibited. Accordingly, we are required faithfully to do what in us lies to defend the life of our neighbor; to promote whatever tends to his tranquility, to be vigilant in warding off harm, and, when danger comes, to assist in removing it.[40]

Calvin believed that the people of God must promote peaceful communities, love others by seeking their protection, and let love guide our actions. It should also guide the policies we advocate, which will offer the protection that love demands. This is hard to do when guns proliferate, as both "Scripture and experience tell us that those who are armed to the teeth cannot build a peaceful society."[41]

Russell Moore, president of the Ethics and Liberty Commission of the Southern Baptist Convention, observes that people long for the type of civic community that is becoming rare in contemporary America. In urban, suburban, and rural areas, there is a lack of real community, of depending on one another, of mutual care and concern. Moore believes, and I agree, that churches must "foster and build real communities built on real love and real truth. These kinds of churches can flourish in rural Oregon and urban Atlanta, in blue states and red states. These kinds of churches can seek to create not just individual disciples, but an alternative order in which the citizens of heaven know one another, trust one another, and are able to call on one another when one hears a strange sound at the window. This will not end the gun control debate, but it can start to bear witness to one of the aspects of this debate we are too afraid to have."[42]

The gospel and the kingdom of God it makes available are for all of us. When he announces his mission in Luke 4, "Jesus proclaims that he has come to preach good news to the poor. As Christians, we must consider what his example means for communities ravaged by gun violence. Chicago mothers are wailing for relief from the violence that is stealing away their children, and, to our shame, it took a massacre in a white suburban elementary school for the nation to hear them. Now that we do, how will we respond to their cries?"[43]

The church, in Chicago and elsewhere, must not only bring the good news to the poor; it must *be* the good news. So, as a church, express support for the policies you think will reduce gun violence. Add positions on guns to your list of criteria for any acceptable political candidate. Write, email, tweet at, or call your representatives and others in government expressing your views. Ask them to act. Be a redemptive presence in your community and the world. Love and care for the widow, the orphan, the marginalized, the victimized, and the vulnerable. Love and serve those in communities ravaged by gun violence by acting to reduce that violence.

One of the most fundamental ways to help build good and safe communities is to help build good and safe families. Fatherlessness and motherlessness leave psychological carnage in their wake. That carnage has social consequences. For example, adolescents whose fathers have never been present in the home are over three times as likely to go to jail as their peers from households where both mother and father are present.[44] The church needs to provide support and care for single parents. It needs to do what it can to hold fathers accountable for being fathers to their children. It needs to put more time and energy into building strong families, within its walls as well as within the community it serves.

Oppose Reverence for the Second Amendment

Christians should be wary about how we talk and think about the US Constitution and the Bill of Rights, including the Second Amendment. Too many appear to revere these writings almost as if they were scriptural. Some equate the authority of the Second Amendment with the authority of the gospel. Those who tend to do this are *Christian nationalists.*

Christian nationalists believe there is an inviolable connection between Christianity and American society. They don't just celebrate the religious faith of the founding fathers. They go further and contend that America has been and should be a Christian nation. This means that American identity, symbols, and policies should reflect a Christian identity. In fact, "for adherents to this ideology, America's historic statements about human liberties (e.g., the First and Second Amendments) are imbued with sacred, literal and absolute meaning."[45] For Christian nationalists, the right to bear arms is a right God grants to Americans. To deny the right is to deny the will of God.

But this is deeply mistaken. The Second Amendment is not on par with the Scriptures. The American Constitution and Bill of Rights are not a revelation from God. America was founded upon beautiful and deeply moral ideals. I am not denigrating the Constitution nor the Bill of Rights. As we have sought to expand the rights and liberties it describes to all Americans, our nation has become better and more just. But for those who are followers of Christ, we must not revere the Constitution. We must not revere the Bill of Rights. We must not revere the Second Amendment. If we do, we violate the second commandment, to have no other gods before God.

Seek Wisdom about God, Guns, and Violence

Last but not least, we must seek wisdom about these issues and then put what we discover into practice. All people of good will want to reduce gun violence. They want fewer innocent people to suffer from it. Often, the disagreements are about how to do this. We need wisdom to find the most effective means of reducing gun violence while protecting the rights of all people. We need the compassion and courage to fight for whatever the best answers turn out to be. I've offered some here, and I deeply hope that we continue to seek more ways to reduce gun violence.

Perhaps one reason that "gun violence is rampant in America is because the subject itself is seldom raised from our pulpits, discussed in [officers] meetings, debated in Sunday school, and considered at our fellowship dinners and pot-luck suppers."[46]

We need sermons that address violence in general and consider applications of the Bible to gun violence in particular. It would be wonderful if pastors across America preached a sermon on Luke 22:35-38, as well as on the many passages in Scripture that condemn violence and call for peace. Perhaps many churches could screen the *Armor of Light* documentary and discuss its implications not just for a Christian view of guns but for what they should do to help solve the problem of gun violence in their community. Rob Schenck, the subject of *Armor of Light*, is the president of the Dietrich Bonhoeffer Institute in Washington, DC. The institute offers a free Bible study—"Fully Protected"—that incorporates part of *Armor of Light*. The study is a resource for those who want to explore what the Bible advises about responding to gun violence.[47] The United Methodist Church also offers a Bible study, *Kingdom Dreams, Violent Realities*, which includes reflections on gun violence grounded in Micah 4:1-4.[48]

Conclusion

As I finish writing this book, a bill has been introduced in Congress to require background checks on private gun sales. The purpose of the Bipartisan Background Checks Act of 2019 is to require the buyer of every firearm sold in America to undergo a background check. Whether it will be put to a vote, much less be voted into law, remains to be seen. Either way, it is clear that there are things we can do to reduce the amount of gun violence in America while also protecting the rights of responsible individuals to own and use certain types of firearms.

Some believe that, given what the Scriptures say about violence, it will be with us until the arrival of the new heavens and the new earth. Given this, they contend that we should—or at least will—go on fighting, shooting, killing, and dying. This, they believe, is a truth we must accept because we live in a fallen world. This makes no more sense than it does to neglect the poor, given Jesus's words that we'll always have the poor with us.

We tend to interpret passages about peace as being about our inner peace. And there is something to this. However, it does not stop there. To think it does is to be held captive to the individualism of our time. The peace of God is not just personal. It is interpersonal. It is social. All swords will not be beaten into plowshares until God's kingdom comes in its fullness. But our lives are to be shaped by that kingdom in the here and now. We can have more plowshares and fewer swords. We can use our capabilities to bring life from the earth rather than put bullet-ridden dead bodies into the earth.

While violence may be with us until the end, and weapons will likely take on ever more lethal forms, Christians should not accept the status quo. Nor should we idolize violence or guns. Instead, we should let the vision of beating swords into plowshares capture our hearts and minds now.

We have no other choice if we want to make the prayer of Jesus not just our prayer but also the guiding force of our lives: "Your kingdom come, your will be done, on earth as it is in heaven."

NOTES

Chapter 1

1. "Heroes Risk Their Lives to Stop Mass Shootings. Lawmakers Don't Have the Guts to Pass Gun Reform," editorial, *Washington Post*, May 8, 2019, https://www.washingtonpost.com/opinions/heroes-risk -their-lives-to-stop-mass-shootings-lawmakers-dont-have-the-guts-to -pass-gun-reform/2019/05/08/990d9abe-71cb-11e9-8be0-ca575670e91c _story.html.

2. Amanda Holpuch, "Columbine at 20: How School Shootings Became 'Part of the American Psyche,'" *Guardian* (US edition), April 17, 2019, https://www.theguardian.com/us-news/2019/apr/17/how -columbine-changed-america-20-year-anniversary-school-shootings.

3. CNN Transcripts, October 29, 2018, http://transcripts.cnn.com /TRANSCRIPTS/1810/29/nday.05.html.

4. Educational Fund to Stop Gun Violence, "New CDC Data Show That Nearly 40,000 People Died by Guns in 2017," news release, December 7, 2018, https://efsgv.org/press-archive/2018/cdc-shows-increase -in-gun-deaths-in-2017/; Jacqueline Howard, "Gun Deaths in US Reach Highest Level in Nearly 40 Years, CDC Data Reveal," *CNN*, December 14, 2018, https://www.cnn.com/2018/12/13/health/gun-deaths-highest -40-years-cdc/index.html.

5. National Center for Statistics and Analysis, "2017 Fatal Motor Vehicle Crashes: Overview," Washington, DC, 2018, https://crashstats .nhtsa.dot.gov/Api/Public/ViewPublication/812603.

6. "Past Summary Ledgers," Gun Violence Archive, accessed July 23, 2019, https://www.gunviolencearchive.org/past-tolls.

7. "Key Gun Violence Statistics," Brady Campaign to Prevent

Gun Violence, accessed July 23, 2019, http://www.bradycampaign.org /key-gun-violence-statistics.

8. Lindsey Tanner, "Guns Send over 8,000 US Kids to ER Each Year, Analysis Says," Associated Press, October 28, 2018, https://www.apnews .com/b806812a8f0945128b4c5e47a9f3c739.

9. Hugh LaFollette, *In Defense of Gun Control* (New York: Oxford University Press, 2018), vii.

10. Jennifer Carlson, *Citizen-Protectors: The Everyday Politics of Guns in an Age of Decline* (New York: Oxford University Press, 2015), 66-67.

11. Pamela Haag, *The Gunning of America* (New York: Basic Books, 2016), xi-xii.

12. Haag, *The Gunning of America*, xii.

13. Haag, *The Gunning of America*, 333.

14. David Brooks, "Guns and the Soul of America," *New York Times*, January 20, 2018, https://www.nytimes.com/2017/10/06/opinion/guns -soul-of-america.html.

15. David Yamane, "The Sociology of U.S. Gun Culture," *Sociology Compass* 11, no. 7 (July 1, 2017): e12497, https://doi.org/10.1111/soc4.12497.

16. "Gun Culture 1.0" and "Gun Culture 2.0" are terms coined by Michael Bane, a journalist and author. For more information, see his blog at http://michaelbane.blogspot.com.

17. Yamane, "The Sociology of U.S. Gun Culture."

18. Carlson, *Citizen-Protectors*, 6.

19. Carlson, *Citizen-Protectors*, 5.

20. Carlson, *Citizen-Protectors*, 66.

21. Yamane, "The Sociology of U.S. Gun Culture."

22. Yamane, "The Sociology of U.S. Gun Culture."

23. Michael Waldman, *The Second Amendment: A Biography* (New York: Simon & Schuster, 2015), xii.

24. Patrick J. Charles, *Armed in America: A History of Gun Rights from Colonial Militias to Concealed Carry* (Amherst, NY: Prometheus, 2018), 41-69.

25. Waldman, *The Second Amendment*, xii.

26. Scott Brinton, "Puckle Gun, AR-15, What's the Difference?," *Long Island Herald*, March 9, 2018, http://www.liherald.com/merrick/stories /puckle-gun-ar-15-whats-the-difference,100973.

27. Waldman, *The Second Amendment*, 27.

28. Waldman, *The Second Amendment*, 60.

29. Waldman, *The Second Amendment*, 63.

30. Waldman, *The Second Amendment*, 63.

31. Scott Rae, *Moral Choices: An Introduction to Ethics*, 4th ed. (Grand Rapids: Zondervan, 2018), 413–15.

32. Rae, *Moral Choices*, 413–15.

33. *McDonald v. City of Chicago, Ill.*, 561 U.S. 742 (2010).

34. *District of Columbia v. Heller*, 554 U.S. 570 (2008).

35. James E. Atwood, *America and Its Guns: A Theological Exposé* (Eugene, OR: Wipf & Stock, 2012), 136–37.

36. Atwood, *America and Its Guns*, 137.

37. Unless otherwise indicated, scriptural references in this book are to the New Revised Standard Version.

38. Joseph Rhee, Tahman Bradley, and Brian Ross, "U.S. Military Weapons Inscribed with Secret 'Jesus' Bible Codes," *ABC News*, January 18, 2010, https://abcnews.go.com/Blotter/us-military-weapons -inscribed-secret-jesus-bible-codes/story?id=9575794.

39. Elicka Peterson Sparks, *The Devil You Know: The Surprising Link between Conservative Christianity and Crime* (Amherst, NY: Prometheus, 2016), 15.

40. Sparks, *The Devil You Know*, 94–96.

41. Jonathan Merritt, "Jerry Falwell Jr.'s Troubling Remarks on Guns," *Atlantic*, December 6, 2015, https://www.theatlantic.com/politics /archive/2015/12/jerry-falwell-jrs-troubling-remarks-on-guns/419019.

42. David Brockman, "Pistol-Packin' Christians," *Texas Observer*, accessed July 23, 2019, https://www.texasobserver.org/pistol-packin -christians/.

43. John Piper, "Should Christians Be Encouraged to Arm Themselves?," *Desiring God*, December 22, 2015, https://www.desiringgod.org /articles/should-christians-be-encouraged-to-arm-themselves.

44. Rob Schenck, *Costly Grace: An Evangelical Minister's Rediscovery of Faith, Hope, and Love* (New York: Harper, 2018).

45. Schenck, *Costly Grace*, 265.

46. Schenck, *Costly Grace*, 266–67.

47. Bruce Reyes-Chow, "Why This Christian Will Never Own a Gun," *Red Letter Christians*, August 30, 2012, https://www.redletterchristians .org/why-this-christian-will-never-own-a-gun/.

48. Shane Claiborne, "Beating AK47s into Shovels," *Huffington Post*, August 15, 2013, updated December 6, 2017, https://www.huffingtonpost .com/shane-claiborne/beating-ak47s-into-shovels_b_3762948.html.

49. The lyrics to "By Degrees" can be found at https://www.by degreessong.com/the-lyrics.

Chapter 2

1. https://www.youtube.com/watch?v=bOJQFNOQqCY.

2. Andrew Fagan, "Human Rights," Internet Encyclopedia of Philosophy, accessed July 23, 2019, http://www.iep.utm.edu/hum-rts/#SH3a.

3. See Emily Badger, "No, You Don't Have an Absolute Right to Own Guns," *Washington Post*, December 7, 2015, https://www.washingtonpost .com/news/wonk/wp/2015/12/07/no-you-dont-have-an-absolute-right -to-own-guns/. She clearly states: "None of our rights work this way."

4. C'Zar Bernstein, Timothy Hsiao, and Matt Palumbo, "The Moral Right to Keep and Bear Firearms," *Public Affairs Quarterly* 29, no. 4 (2015): 345–63.

5. This argument parallels an argument for the morality of war in Brian Orend, *The Morality of War*, 2nd ed. (Peterborough, ON, and Buffalo: Broadview, 2013), 40–41.

6. David DeGrazia and Lester H. Hunt, *Debating Gun Control: How Much Regulation Do We Need?* (New York: Oxford University Press, 2016), 148–71.

7. DeGrazia and Hunt, *Debating Gun Control*, 164–65.

8. Michael Huemer, "Is There a Right to Own a Gun?," *Social Theory and Practice* 29, no. 2 (2003): 297–324.

9. Caroline Light, *Stand Your Ground: A History of America's Love Affair with Lethal Self-Defense* (Boston: Beacon, 2017), 8.

10. "The 2018 Florida Statutes," Sunshine Online, accessed July 23, 2019, http://www.leg.state.fl.us/Statutes/index.cfm?App_mode =Display_Statute&URL=0700-0799/0776/0776.html.

11. Light, *Stand Your Ground*, 10, 16.

12. Ta-Nehisi Coates, "Stand Your Ground and Vigilante Justice," *Atlantic*, March 22, 2012, http://www.theatlantic.com/national /archive/2012/03/stand-your-ground-and-vigilante-justice/254900/.

Chapter 3

1. See Gregory Bassham et al., *Critical Thinking: A Student's Introduction*, 5th ed. (New York: McGraw-Hill, 2012), chaps. 5–6.

2. Philip J. Cook and Kristin A. Goss, *The Gun Debate: What Everyone Needs to Know* (Oxford: Oxford University Press, 2014), 34–42; Matthew Miller, Deborah Azrael, and David Hemenway, "Firearms and Violent Death in the United States," in *Reducing Gun Violence in America: Informing Policy with Evidence and Analysis*, ed. Daniel W. Webster and Jon S. Vernick (Baltimore: Johns Hopkins University Press, 2013), 3–20.

3. Cook and Goss, *The Gun Debate*, 42.

4. Miller, Azrael, and Hemenway, "Firearms and Violent Death," 3–20.

5. Miller, Azrael, and Hemenway, "Firearms and Violent Death," 12.

6. Miller, Azrael, and Hemenway, "Firearms and Violent Death," 13.

7. David B. Kopel, *The Morality of Self-Defense and Military Action: The Judeo-Christian Tradition* (Santa Barbara, CA, and Denver: Praeger, 2017), 414.

8. "Police: Masked Gunman Killed by Alabama McDonald's Customer," Associated Press, October 29, 2018, https://apnews.com/86e53d649683429188b3e3f79dd398b8.

9. "Firearm Justifiable Homicides and Non-Fatal Self-Defense Gun Use: An Analysis of Federal Bureau of Investigation and National Crime Victimization Survey Data," Violence Policy Center, May 2017.

10. Cook and Goss, *The Gun Debate*, 185–88, 190–202.

11. Jake Novak, "Stop Blaming the NRA for Failed Gun Control Efforts," *CNBC*, February 16, 2018, https://www.cnbc.com/2018/02/16/nra-money-isnt-why-gun-control-efforts-are-failing-commentary.html.

12. Cook and Goss, *The Gun Debate*, 192–202.

13. Cook and Goss, *The Gun Debate*, 198–202.

14. Jeremy Diamond and Tom LoBianco, "Donald Trump: Obama Considering Executive Order to Take Guns Away," *CNN*, October 20, 2015, https://www.cnn.com/2015/10/19/politics/donald-trump-guns-obama-south-carolina/index.html.

15. Jason Le Miere, "Wayne LaPierre Slams 'Elites' in CPAC Speech Even as He Earns $5 Million Annually from NRA," *Newsweek*, February 22, 2018, http://www.newsweek.com/wayne-lapierre-nra-cpac-guns-816294.

16. Max Ehrenfreund, "Why So Many Americans Think the Government Wants Their Guns," *Washington Post*, January 8, 2016, https://

www.washingtonpost.com/news/wonk/wp/2016/01/08/why-so-many
-americans-think-the-government-wants-their-guns/.

17. Bassham et al., *Critical Thinking*, 151.

18. "John Paul Stevens: Repeal the Second Amendment," *New York Times*, March 28, 2018, https://www.nytimes.com/2018/03/27/opinion
/john-paul-stevens-repeal-second-amendment.html.

19. Mike Huckabee, *God, Guns, Grits, and Gravy* (New York: St. Martin's Griffin, 2016), 20.

20. David Kyle Johnson, "Fallacy: All or Nothing," in *Bad Arguments: 100 of the Most Important Fallacies in Western Philosophy*, ed. Robert Arp, Steven Barbone, and Michael Bruce (Oxford: Wiley Blackwell, 2018). Available at https://www.academia.edu/21565174/Fallacy_All_or_Nothing.

21. Huckabee, *God, Guns, Grits, and Gravy*, 23.

22. Euan McKirdy and Emanuella Grinberg, "Japan Knife Attack: At Least 19 Dead," *CNN*, updated July 26, 2016, https://www.cnn
.com/2016/07/25/world/japan-knife-attack-deaths/index.html.

23. David Harsanyi, "Why Bringing a Gun to Church Is a Pretty Good Idea," *Federalist*, November 7, 2017, http://thefederalist.com/2017/11/07
/bringing-gun-church-pretty-good-idea/.

24. "11 Times a Good Guy with a Gun Stopped a Bad Guy, Saving Lives," photo gallery, *Washington Times*, accessed July 23, 2019, https://www.washingtontimes.com/multimedia/collection/good
-guy-gun-stopped-bad-guy-gun/.

25. "Firearm Justifiable Homicides and Non-Fatal Self-Defense Gun Use."

26. Erin Curry, "Hostage Reads 'Purpose-Driven Life' to Alleged Atlanta Killer," *Baptist Press*, March 14, 2005, http://www.bpnews
.net/20340/hostage-reads-purposedriven-life-to-alleged-atlanta-killer.

27. Holly Yan, "Hero Customer Rushes Waffle House Killer and Rips Away His Assault-Style Rifle," *CNN*, April 23, 2018, https://cnn
philippines.com/world/2018/04/23/Waffle-House-hero.html.

28. "Concealed Carry Killers," Violence Policy Center: Concealed Carry Killers, accessed July 23, 2019, http://concealedcarrykillers.org/.

29. David Hemenway, *Private Guns, Public Health*, rev. ed. (Ann Arbor: University of Michigan Press, 2017), 70–71.

30. Meghan Keneally, "Breaking Down the NRA-Backed Theory That a Good Guy with a Gun Stops a Bad Guy with a Gun," *ABC News*,

October 29, 2018, http://abcnews.go.com/US/breaking-nra-backed
-theory-good-guy-gun-stops/story?id=53360480.

31. Keneally, "Breaking Down the NRA-Backed Theory That a Good Guy with a Gun Stops a Bad Guy with a Gun."

32. Matthew Haag, "Man Killed by Police at Alabama Mall Was a 'Good Guy with a Gun,' Family's Lawyer Says," *New York Times*, November 26, 2018, https://www.nytimes.com/2018/11/26/us/black-man-killed
-alabama-mall-shooting.html.

33. Rob Schenck, *Costly Grace: An Evangelical Minister's Rediscovery of Faith, Hope, and Love* (New York: Harper, 2018), 272.

34. Gary Kleck and Marc Gertz, "Armed Resistance to Crime: The Prevalence and Nature of Self-Defense with a Gun," *Journal of Criminal Law and Criminology* 86, no. 1 (1995): 150–87.

35. Hemenway, *Private Guns, Public Health*, 64–78.

36. Hemenway, *Private Guns, Public Health*, 78.

37. Firmin DeBrabander, *Do Guns Make Us Free? Democracy and the Armed Society* (New Haven: Yale University Press, 2015), 142. In this section I draw from this excellent book. Hereafter, page references from this work will be given in parentheses in the text.

38. "Greene County, Virginia GOP Group's Newsletter Calls for 'Armed Revolution' If Obama Is Reelected," *Huffington Post*, May 8, 2012, updated December 6, 2017, https://www.huffingtonpost.com/2012/05
/08/greene-county-virginia-gop-obama-revolution_n_1501510.html.

39. Huckabee, *God, Guns, Grits, and Gravy*, 29.

40. Cook and Goss, *The Gun Debate*, 30.

41. Kirsten Powers and Jonathan Merritt, "Christians, Guns and the Mass Shooting Epidemic," *The Faith Angle* (podcast), *Relevant*, April 3, 2018, https://relevantmagazine.com/podcast/christians-guns-mass
-shooting-epidemic/.

42. Andrew P. Napolitano, "Guns and Freedom," *Fox News*, January 10, 2013, last updated May 11, 2015, https://www.foxnews.com/opinion
/guns-and-freedom.

43. Huckabee, *God, Guns, Grits, and Gravy*, 29–31.

44. Cook and Goss, *The Gun Debate*, 171–75.

45. Cook and Goss, *The Gun Debate*, 172.

46. Daniel Polsby and Don Kates, "Of Holocausts and Gun Control," *Washington University Law Quarterly* 75 (1997): 1237–75.

47. Polsby and Kates, "Of Holocausts and Gun Control," 1238.

48. Polsby and Kates, "Of Holocausts and Gun Control," 1240.

49. Wayne Grudem, *Christian Ethics: An Introduction to Biblical Moral Reasoning* (Wheaton, IL: Crossway, 2018), 430.

50. Cook and Goss, *The Gun Debate*, 33.

Chapter 4

1. Charles Marsh, "The NRA's Assault on Christian Faith and Practice," *Religion & Politics*, January 3, 2018, http://religionandpolitics .org/2018/01/03/the-nras-assault-on-christian-faith-and-practice/.

2. Kim Parker et al., "America's Complex Relationship with Guns," Pew Research Center, June 22, 2017, https://www.pewsocialtrends .org/2017/06/22/americas-complex-relationship-with-guns/.

3. Eliza Relman, "Megachurch Pastor on 'Fox & Friends' Says His Parishioners Could Stop a Shooting Because They Carry Guns into Church," *Business Insider*, November 6, 2017, https://www.businessinsider .com/megachurch-pastor-fox-friends-guns-concealed-carry-2017-11.

4. Jonathan Merritt, "Jerry Falwell Jr.'s Troubling Remarks on Guns," *Atlantic*, December 6, 2015, https://www.theatlantic.com/politics /archive/2015/12/jerry-falwell-jrs-troubling-remarks-on-guns/419019/.

5. Athanasius, *On the Incarnation of the Word* 8.52, https://www.ccel .org/ccel/athanasius/incarnation.ix.html.

6. Marsh, "The NRA's Assault on Christian Faith and Practice."

7. "Martin Luther King Jr.—Acceptance Speech," Nobel Prize, December 10, 1964, https://www.nobelprize.org/prizes/peace/1964 /king/26142-martin-luther-king-jr-acceptance-speech-1964/.

8. Paul N. Anderson, "Jesus and Peace," *Faculty Publications—College of Christian Studies* 96 (1994), http://digitalcommons.georgefox.edu/ccs/96.

9. Anderson, "Jesus and Peace."

10. Tim Suttle, "Why Do American Christians Trust the 2nd Amendment More Than the Sermon on the Mount?," *Patheos*, July 9, 2016, https://www.patheos.com/blogs/paperbacktheology/2016/07/why-do -american-christians-trust-the-2nd-amendment-more-than-the-sermon -on-the-mount.html.

11. Scott Rae, *Moral Choices: An Introduction to Ethics*, 4th ed. (Grand Rapids: Zondervan, 2018), 299–307.

12. For more on this, see Paul Copan and Matt Flannagan, *Did God Really Command Genocide? Coming to Terms with the Justice of God* (Grand Rapids: Baker Books, 2014).

13. Rae, *Moral Choices*, 409–10.

14. Wayne Grudem, *Christian Ethics: An Introduction to Biblical Moral Reasoning* (Wheaton, IL: Crossway, 2018), 526–33.

15. Relman, "Megachurch Pastor on 'Fox & Friends' Says His Parishioners Could Stop a Shooting Because They Carry Guns into Church."

16. Rae, *Moral Choices*, 410–12.

17. Richard B. Hays, *The Moral Vision of the New Testament: Community, Cross, New Creation; A Contemporary Introduction to New Testament Ethics* (San Francisco: HarperOne, 1996), 336.

18. Roland H. Bainton, *Christian Attitudes toward War and Peace: A Historical Survey and Critical Re-evaluation* (New York: Abingdon, 1960), 242.

19. Christopher A. Hall, *Living Wisely with the Church Fathers* (Downers Grove, IL: IVP Academic, 2017), 93–127.

20. Lactantius, *Divine Institutes*, book 4, chap. 20, New Advent, accessed July 23, 2019, http://www.newadvent.org/fathers/07016.htm.

21. Hall, *Living Wisely*, 116.

22. Robertson McQuilkin and Paul Copan, *An Introduction to Biblical Ethics: Walking in the Way of Wisdom*, 3rd ed. (Downers Grove, IL: IVP Academic, 2014), 350.

23. Rae, *Moral Choices*, 302.

24. Joseph Quinn Raab, "Comrades for Peace: Thomas Merton, the Dalai Lama and the Preferential Option for Nonviolence," *Merton Annual* 19 (2006): 263.

25. Marsh, "The NRA's Assault on Christian Faith and Practice."

26. Dallas Willard, *The Divine Conspiracy: Rediscovering Our Hidden Life in God* (San Francisco: Harper, 1998).

27. Willard, *The Divine Conspiracy*, 25.

28. Glen Stassen and David Gushee, *Kingdom Ethics: Following Jesus in Contemporary Context* (Downers Grove, IL: IVP Academic, 2003), 147.

29. Mark Galli, "God Hates Gun Violence," *Christianity Today*, May 18, 2018, https://www.christianitytoday.com/ct/2018/june/god-hates -gun-violence.html.

30. For a discussion of violence and the Old Testament, see Matthew

Curtis Fleischer, *The Old Testament Case for Nonviolence* (Oklahoma City: Epic Octavius the Triumphant, 2017).

31. Hays, *The Moral Vision*, 332.

32. Grudem, *Christian Ethics*, 557.

33. Philip J. Cook and Kristin A. Goss, *The Gun Debate: What Everyone Needs to Know* (Oxford: Oxford University Press, 2014), 43.

34. David Hemenway, *Private Guns, Public Health*, rev. ed. (Ann Arbor: University of Michigan Press, 2017), 123–24.

35. Cook and Goss, *The Gun Debate*, 43, 145–46.

36. Grudem, *Christian Ethics*, 551–52, 557.

37. Hays, *The Moral Vision*, 319–37.

38. Hays, *The Moral Vision*, 326.

39. Hays, *The Moral Vision*, 326.

40. Willard, *The Divine Conspiracy*, 132–37.

41. Willard, *The Divine Conspiracy*, 175–83.

42. Willard, *The Divine Conspiracy*, 176.

43. Willard, *The Divine Conspiracy*, 179–80.

44. Marsh, "The NRA's Assault on Christian Faith and Practice."

45. Francie Diep, "Church Shootings Are Becoming Much More Common," *Pacific Standard*, November 6, 2017, https://psmag.com /news/church-shootings-are-becoming-much-more-common.

46. Mira Hutchinson, "Mike Huckabee: If Only Someone in That Church Had Been Carrying a Gun Too," *Hinterland Gazette*, June 19, 2015, https://hinterlandgazette.com/2015/06/mike-huckabee-charleston -church-shooting-concealed-weapon.html.

47. Jack Jenkins, "Lawmakers Calling for More Guns in Church Have a Theology Problem," *Think Progress*, November 6, 2017, https://think progress.org/guns-church-theology-problem-0cde29cf72f8/.

48. Jenkins, "Lawmakers Calling for More Guns in Church Have a Theology Problem."

49. Kevin J. Farrell, "A Response to Open Carry," Bishop Kevin Farrell, January 5, 2016, https://bishopkevinfarrell.org/2016/01/open-carry/.

50. Jenkins, "Lawmakers Calling for More Guns in Church Have a Theology Problem."

51. Emily Shapiro, "During Discussion about Guns in Church, Man Accidentally Shoots Himself, Wife: Police," *ABC News*, November 17,

2017, https://abcnews.go.com/US/man-accidentally-shoots-wife-church -discussing-weapons-churches/story?id=51221000.

52. Alicia Fabbre and Vikki Ortiz Healy, "Pastor's Son Accidentally Shoots, Kills Teen Cousin in Will County; Police Say No Charges Expected," *Chicago Tribune*, December 27, 2018, https://www.chicagotribune .com/suburbs/ct-met-juvenile-shot-willmington-church-20171227-story .html.

53. Megan Briggs, "Pastor, Will You Allow Guns in Your Church?," *Church Leaders*, November 8, 2017, https://churchleaders.com/news /culture/312955-pastor-will-allow-guns-church.html.

54. Kimberly Johnson, "Carolina Congregations Wrestle with Taking Guns to Church," *Aljazeera America*, August 31, 2015, http://america .aljazeera.com/articles/2015/8/31/carolina-guns-in-churches.html.

Chapter 5

1. "Gun Control and the Bible," Conservative Christians of Alabama, accessed July 23, 2019, http://www.ccofal.org/alabama/what-does-the -bible-verses-say-about-gun-control.html.

2. Drawing here upon Craig S. Keener, *The Gospel of Matthew: A Socio-Rhetorical Commentary* (Grand Rapids: Eerdmans, 2009), 329–31.

3. Robertson McQuilkin and Paul Copan, *An Introduction to Biblical Ethics: Walking in the Way of Wisdom*, 3rd ed. (Downers Grove, IL: IVP Academic, 2014), 417.

4. Andy Alexis-Baker, "Violence, Nonviolence and the Temple Incident in John 2:13–15," *Biblical Interpretation* 20, no. 1–2 (2012): 73–96.

5. Alexis-Baker, "Violence, Nonviolence," 74.

6. David Rensberger, "Jesus's Action in the Temple," in *Struggles for Shalom: Peace and Violence across the Testaments*, ed. Laura L. Brenneman and Brad D. Schantz (Eugene, OR: Pickwick, 2014), 179–90.

7. Rensberger, "Jesus's Action in the Temple," 183.

8. Alexis-Baker, "Violence, Nonviolence," 94.

9. Thomas R. Yoder Neufeld, *Killing Enmity: Violence and the New Testament* (Grand Rapids: Baker Academic, 2011), 61.

10. Neufeld, *Killing Enmity*, 70.

11. Cf. David J. Neville, *The Vehement Jesus: Grappling with Troubling Gospel Texts* (Eugene, OR: Cascade, 2017), 179.

12. Rensberger, "Jesus's Action in the Temple," 189.

13. Abigail Disney, *The Armor of Light*, documentary (Samuel Goldwyn Films, 2015).

14. David Hemenway, "Does Owning a Gun Make You Safer?," *Los Angeles Times*, August 4, 2015, http://www.latimes.com/opinion/op-ed /la-oe-0804-hemenway-defensive-gun-home-20150730-story.html.

15. Michael W. Austin and Ron Gleason, "The Gun Control Debate: Two Christian Perspectives," *Christian Research Journal* 36, no. 6 (2013): 23.

16. Steve Cable, "A Christian Worldview Appraisal of Gun Control and the Second Amendment," *Probe for Answers*, September 5, 2015, https://probe.org/a-christian-worldview-appraisal-of-gun-control-and -the-second-amendment/.

17. Joel B. Green, Scot McKnight, and I. Howard Marshall, eds., *Dictionary of Jesus and the Gospels* (Downers Grove, IL: IVP Academic, 1992), 495, 498–502.

18. Wayne A. Grudem, *Politics according to the Bible: A Comprehensive Resource for Understanding Modern Political Issues in Light of Scripture* (Grand Rapids: Zondervan, 2010), 194, 202–3.

19. Joel B. Green, *The Gospel of Luke*, New International Commentary on the New Testament (Grand Rapids: Eerdmans, 1997), 774. Others who argue for the symbolic interpretation include Darrell L. Bock, *Luke 9:51–24:53*, 3rd ed. (Grand Rapids: Baker Academic, 1996); James R. Edwards, *The Gospel according to Luke* (Grand Rapids: Eerdmans, 2015); and I. Howard Marshall, *The Gospel of Luke*, American ed. (Grand Rapids: Eerdmans, 1978).

20. Advocates of this interpretation, from which the following is drawn, include Joseph A. Fitzmyer, *The Gospel according to Luke X–XXIV: Introduction, Translation, and Notes* (Garden City, NY: Doubleday, 1985); G. W. H. Lampe, "The Two Swords (Luke 22:35–38)," in *Jesus and the Politics of His Day*, ed. Ernst Bammel and C. F. D. Moule (Cambridge: Cambridge University Press, 1984), 335–51; Paul Minear, "A Note on Luke XXII 36," *Novum Testamentum* 7 (1964): 128–34; and Neville, *The Vehement Jesus*.

21. Lampe, "The Two Swords (Luke 22:35–38)," 341–42, 347.

22. Neville, *The Vehement Jesus*, 106.

23. Minear, "A Note on Luke XXII 36," 131.

24. Moyer Hubbard, "'Let the One Who Has No Sword, Buy One':

The Biblical Argument for Gun Control, Part Two," *Good Book Blog,* February 25, 2014, https://www.biola.edu/blogs/good-book-blog/2014 /let-the-one-who-has-no-sword-buy-one-the-biblical-argument-for -gun-control-part-two.

Chapter 6

1. Dallas Willard, *Renovation of the Heart: Putting On the Character of Christ* (Colorado Springs: NavPress, 2002), 15.

2. Dallas Willard, *The Divine Conspiracy: Rediscovering Our Hidden Life in God* (San Francisco: Harper, 1998), chap. 5.

3. Rob Schenck, *Costly Grace: An Evangelical Minister's Rediscovery of Faith, Hope, and Love* (New York: Harper, 2018), 270.

4. Schenck, *Costly Grace,* 270.

5. Richard Lacayo, "Under Fire," *Time,* June 24, 2001, http://content .time.com/time/magazine/article/0,9171,153695,00.html.

6. Charles Marsh, "The NRA's Assault on Christian Faith and Practice," *Religion & Politics,* January 3, 2018, http://religionandpolitics .org/2018/01/03/the-nras-assault-on-christian-faith-and-practice/.

7. James E. Atwood, *America and Its Guns: A Theological Exposé* (Eugene, OR: Wipf & Stock, 2012), 19–25.

8. Shane Claiborne and Michael Martin, *Beating Guns: Hope for People Who Are Weary of Violence* (Grand Rapids: Brazos, 2019), 192.

9. Claiborne and Martin, *Beating Guns,* 158.

10. Claiborne and Martin, *Beating Guns,* 192.

11. P. Andrew Sandlin, posting for Bill Blankschaen, "Pistol Packin' Jesus: A Response to Shane Claiborne," *Patheos,* December 15, 2015, https://www.patheos.com/blogs/faithwalkers/2015/12/pistol-packin -jesus-a-response-to-shane-claiborne/.

12. See the discussion of this text in chapter 5.

13. Wayne Grudem, *Christian Ethics: An Introduction to Biblical Moral Reasoning* (Wheaton, IL: Crossway, 2018), 537.

14. Scott Rae, *Moral Choices: An Introduction to Ethics,* 4th ed. (Grand Rapids: Zondervan, 2018), 410.

15. Richard B. Hays, *The Moral Vision of the New Testament: Community, Cross, New Creation; A Contemporary Introduction to New Testament Ethics* (San Francisco: HarperOne, 1996), 173–79.

16. Romano Guardini, *The Lord* (Washington, DC: Gateway Editions, 1996), 612.

17. Pamela Haag, *The Gunning of America* (New York: Basic Books, 2016), 181–82.

18. What follows draws from a discussion of military training, but the parallels with Gun Culture 2.0 are made clear. See Franco Trivigno, "A Virtue Ethical Case for Pacifism," in *Virtues in Action: New Essays in Applied Virtue Ethics*, ed. Michael W. Austin (New York: Palgrave Macmillan, 2013), 86–101.

19. Trivigno, "A Virtue Ethical Case," 87.

20. David Livingstone Smith, *Less Than Human: Why We Demean, Enslave, and Exterminate Others* (New York: St. Martin's, 2011).

21. Kat Ainsworth, "I Call Shotgun: The Rolling Thunder Drill," Truth about Guns, August 12, 2018, https://www.thetruthaboutguns .com/2018/08/kat-ainsworth/i-call-shotgun-the-rolling-thunder-drill/.

22. David Yamane, "A Counterargument to 'Virtue and Guns,'" *Psychology Today*, May 24, 2019, https://www.psychologytoday.com/blog /ethics-everyone/201905/counterargument-virtue-and-guns.

23. Trivigno, "A Virtue Ethical Case," 93.

24. Chris Williams, "The Strange Love Affair between Christians and Guns," *Patheos*, June 14, 2016, https://www.patheos.com/blogs /chrisicisms/2016/06/14/christians-and-guns/.

25. Bruce Handy, "'The Armor of Light' Is a Documentary That Explores the Intersection of Christianity and Guns," *Vanity Fair*, November 16, 2015, https://www.vanityfair.com/hollywood/2015/11 /the-armor-of-light-documentary-christianity-guns.

26. In this section, I draw from Rebecca Konyndyk DeYoung's description of courage in her "Courage," in *Being Good: Christian Virtues for Everyday Life*, ed. Michael W. Austin and R. Douglas Geivett (Grand Rapids: Eerdmans, 2012), 145–66.

27. DeYoung, "Courage," 147.

28. DeYoung, "Courage," 163.

29. DeYoung, "Courage," 164.

30. DeYoung, "Courage," 154.

31. "In Guns We Trust," editorial, *Christianity Today*, October 4, 1999, https://www.christianitytoday.com/ct/1999/october4/in-guns-we-trust -fear-idolatry.html.

Chapter 7

1. Mark Leibovich, "Do Politicians' 'Thoughts and Prayers' Mean Anything?," *New York Times*, January 19, 2018, https://www.nytimes.com/2015/10/18/magazine/do-politicians-thoughts-and-prayers-mean-anything.html.

2. Katie Reilly, "'Thoughts and Prayers Are Not Enough.' Democrats Demand Action after Texas Shooting," *Time*, November 6, 2017, http://time.com/5011550/texas-church-shooting-thoughts-prayers-gun-control/.

3. John Cheves, "A Boy Finds His Father's Loaded Gun. Why Doesn't Dad Go to Jail When Someone Dies?," *Lexington (KY) Herald-Leader*, July 21, 2017, updated August 14, 2018, http://www.kentucky.com/news/local/watchdog/article162848728.html.

4. Elicka Peterson Sparks, *The Devil You Know: The Surprising Link between Conservative Christianity and Crime* (Amherst, NY: Prometheus, 2016), 104.

5. Ramin Skibba, "Researchers Tackle Gun Violence Despite Lack of Federal Funding," *NPR*, May 12, 2018, https://www.npr.org/sections/health-shots/2018/05/12/609701029/researchers-tackle-gun-violence-despite-lack-of-federal-funding.

6. Hugh LaFollette, *In Defense of Gun Control* (New York: Oxford University Press, 2018), 136–89.

7. Shall-issue laws require a state to issue a concealed-carry license unless there is a demonstrable reason to deny this right.

8. LaFollette, *In Defense of Gun Control*, 156–57.

9. Philip J. Cook and Kristin A. Goss, *The Gun Debate: What Everyone Needs to Know* (Oxford: Oxford University Press, 2014). Interested readers may also want to consult LaFollette, *In Defense of Gun Control*; Daniel W. Webster and Jon S. Vernick, eds., *Reducing Gun Violence in America: Informing Policy with Evidence and Analysis* (Baltimore: Johns Hopkins University Press, 2013); and John R. Lott, *More Guns, Less Crime: Understanding Crime and Gun Control Laws*, 3rd ed. (Chicago: University of Chicago Press, 2010).

10. Michael W. Austin and Ron Gleason, "The Gun Control Debate: Two Christian Perspectives," *Christian Research Journal* 36, no. 6 (2013): 12–23.

11. Daniel W. Webster and Jon S. Vernick, "Spurring Responsible Firearms Sales Practice through Litigation," in Webster and Vernick, *Reducing Gun Violence in America*, 21–32.

12. Philip J. Cook and Jens Ludwig, "The Limited Impact of the Brady Act," in Webster and Vernick, *Reducing Gun Violence in America*, 21–32.

13. Garen J. Wintemute, "Broadening Denial Criteria for the Purchase and Possession of Firearms," in Webster and Vernick, *Reducing Gun Violence in America*, 77–93.

14. Lott, *More Guns, Less Crime*, 164–66.

15. See Firmin DeBrabander, *Do Guns Make Us Free? Democracy and the Armed Society* (New Haven: Yale University Press, 2015), 144–58.

16. LaFollette, *In Defense of Gun Control*, 145–47, 178–84.

17. LaFollette, *In Defense of Gun Control*, 181.

18. LaFollette, *In Defense of Gun Control*, 184.

19. DeBrabander, *Do Guns Make Us Free?*, 157–58.

20. DeBrabander, *Do Guns Make Us Free?*, 157–58.

21. Austin and Gleason, "The Gun Control Debate."

22. "Study Finds States with Most Gun Laws Have Fewest Gun Deaths But . . . ," *WBUR* (Boston), March 13, 2013, https://www.wbur.org/hereandnow/2013/03/13/gun-laws-study.

23. LaFollette, *In Defense of Gun Control*, 192–93.

24. Webster and Vernick, *Reducing Gun Violence in America*, 260–61.

25. Webster and Vernick, *Reducing Gun Violence in America*, 260–61.

26. Luke Broadwater, "Sheriff: Maryland's 'Red Flag' Law Prompted Gun Seizures after Four 'Significant Threats' against Schools," *Baltimore Sun*, January 15, 2019, https://www.baltimoresun.com/news/maryland/politics/bs-md-red-flag-update-20190115-story.html.

27. Cook and Goss, *The Gun Debate*, 128–31.

28. Cook and Goss, *The Gun Debate*, 130.

29. Cook and Goss, *The Gun Debate*, 131; LaFollette, *In Defense of Gun Control*, 204.

30. Cook and Goss, *The Gun Debate*, 131.

31. David DeGrazia, "Handguns, Moral Rights, and Physical Security," *Journal of Moral Philosophy* 13 (2014): 1–21.

32. Cook and Goss, *The Gun Debate*, 15.

33. Webster and Vernick, *Reducing Gun Violence in America*, 262.

34. LaFollette, *In Defense of Gun Control*, 210–21.

35. Webster and Vernick, *Reducing Gun Violence in America*, 262.

36. C. S. Lewis, *Mere Christianity*, revised and enlarged ed. (San Francisco: HarperOne, 2015), 177.

37. Dallas Willard, *The Divine Conspiracy: Rediscovering Our Hidden Life in God* (San Francisco: Harper, 1998).

38. Bernard Howard, "A Christian Case for Gun Control," *Mere Orthodoxy*, June 22, 2016, https://mereorthodoxy.com/christian-case-gun-control/.

39. Rita Nakashima Brock and Rebecca Ann Parker, *Proverbs of Ashes: Violence, Redemptive Suffering, and the Search for What Saves Us* (Boston: Beacon, 2002), 20–21.

40. John Calvin, *Institutes of the Christian Religion*, trans. Henry Beveridge, 2.8.39, http://www.ccel.org/ccel/calvin/institutes.iv.ix.html.

41. Atwood, *America and Its Guns*, 213.

42. Russell Moore, "Is Gun Control a Christian Issue?" Russell Moore, January 5, 2016, https://www.russellmoore.com/2016/01/05/is-gun-control-a-christian-issue/.

43. Sharon Hodde Miller, "Why All Christians Can Back Better Gun Control," *Christianity Today*, January 9, 2013, https://www.christianitytoday.com/women/2013/january/why-all-christians-can-back-better-gun-control.html.

44. Cynthia Harper and Sara McLanahan, "Father Absence and Youth Incarceration," *Journal of Research on Adolescence* 14 (2004): 369–97.

45. Andrew Whitehead, Landon Schnabel, and Samuel Perry, "Why Some Christians Don't Believe in Gun Control: They Think God Handed Down the Second Amendment," *Washington Post*, July 25, 2018, https://www.washingtonpost.com/news/acts-of-faith/wp/2018/07/25/why-some-christians-dont-believe-in-gun-control-they-think-god-handed-down-the-second-amendment/.

46. Atwood, *America and Its Guns*, 207.

47. "Fully Protected Bible Study," Dietrich Bonhoeffer Institute, accessed July 23, 2019, https://tdbi.org/resources/fully-protected-bible-study/.

48. Available at https://www.umcjustice.org/what-you-can-do/advocacy/resource-kingdom-dreams-violent-realities-bible-study.

BIBLIOGRAPHY

Ainsworth, Kat. "I Call Shotgun: The Rolling Thunder Drill." Truth about Guns, August 12, 2018. https://www.thetruthaboutguns .com/2018/08/kat-ainsworth/i-call-shotgun-the-rolling-thunder -drill/.

Alexis-Baker, Andy. "Violence, Nonviolence and the Temple Incident in John 2:13–15." *Biblical Interpretation* 20, no. 1–2 (2012): 73–96.

Anderson, Paul N. "Jesus and Peace." *Faculty Publications—College of Christian Studies* 96 (1994). http://digitalcommons.georgefox.edu /ccs/96.

Arp, Robert, Steven Barbone, and Michael Bruce, eds. *Bad Arguments: 100 of the Most Important Fallacies in Western Philosophy*. Oxford: Wiley Blackwell, 2018.

Atwood, James E. *America and Its Guns: A Theological Exposé*. Eugene, OR: Wipf & Stock, 2012.

Austin, M., ed. *Virtues in Action: New Essays in Applied Virtue Ethics*. New York: Palgrave Macmillan, 2013.

Austin, Michael W., and Ron Gleason. "The Gun Control Debate: Two Christian Perspectives." *Christian Research Journal* 36, no. 6 (2013): 12–23.

Badger, Emily. "No, You Don't Have an Absolute Right to Own Guns." *Washington Post*, December 7, 2015. https://www.washingtonpost .com/news/wonk/wp/2015/12/07/no-you-dont-have-an-absolute -right-to-own-guns/.

Bainton, Roland H. *Christian Attitudes toward War and Peace: A Historical Survey and Critical Re-evaluation*. New York: Abingdon, 1960.

Bassham, Gregory, William Irwin, Henry Nardone, and James M. Wallace. *Critical Thinking: A Student's Introduction*. 5th ed. New York: McGraw-Hill, 2012.

Bernstein, C'Zar, Timothy Hsiao, and Matt Palumbo. "The Moral Right to Keep and Bear Firearms." *Public Affairs Quarterly* 29, no. 4 (2015): 345–63.

Bock, Darrell L. *Luke 9:51–24:53*. 3rd ed. Grand Rapids: Baker Academic, 1996.

Briggs, Megan. "Pastor, Will You Allow Guns in Your Church?" *Church Leaders*, November 8, 2017. https://churchleaders.com/news/cul ture/312955-pastor-will-allow-guns-church.html.

Brinton, Scott. "Puckle Gun, AR-15, What's the Difference?" *Long Island Herald*, March 9, 2018. http://www.liherald.com/merrick/stories /puckle-gun-ar-15-whats-the-difference,100973.

Broadwater, Luke. "Sheriff: Maryland's 'Red Flag' Law Prompted Gun Seizures after Four 'Significant Threats' against Schools." *Baltimore Sun*, January 15, 2019. https://www.baltimoresun.com/news /maryland/politics/bs-md-red-flag-update-20190115-story.html.

Brock, Rita Nakashima, and Rebecca Ann Parker. *Proverbs of Ashes: Violence, Redemptive Suffering, and the Search for What Saves Us*. Boston: Beacon, 2002.

Brockman, David. "Pistol-Packin' Christians." *Texas Observer*. Accessed July 23, 2019. https://www.texasobserver.org/pistol-packin-chris tians/.

Brooks, David. "Guns and the Soul of America." *New York Times*, January 20, 2018. https://www.nytimes.com/2017/10/06/opinion /guns-soul-of-america.html.

Cable, Steve. "A Christian Worldview Appraisal of Gun Control and the Second Amendment." *Probe for Answers*, September 5, 2015. https://probe.org/a-christian-worldview-appraisal-of-gun-con trol-and-the-second-amendment/.

Calvin, John. *Institutes of the Christian Religion*. Translated by Henry Beveridge. http://www.ccel.org/ccel/calvin/institutes.iv.ix.html.

Carlson, Jennifer. *Citizen-Protectors: The Everyday Politics of Guns in an Age of Decline*. New York: Oxford University Press, 2015.

Charles, Patrick J. *Armed in America: A History of Gun Rights from Colonial Militias to Concealed Carry*. Amherst, NY: Prometheus, 2018.

Cheves, John. "A Boy Finds His Father's Loaded Gun. Why Doesn't Dad Go to Jail When Someone Dies?" *Lexington (KY) Herald-Leader*,

July 21, 2017, updated August 14, 2018. http://www.kentucky.com
/news/local/watchdog/article162848728.html.

Claiborne, Shane. "Beating AK47s into Shovels." *Huffington Post*, August
15, 2013, updated December 6, 2017. https://www.huffingtonpost
.com/shane-claiborne/beating-ak47s-into-shovels_b_3762948.html.

———. "Jerry Falwell Jr. Is Wrong to Encourage Concealed Weapons to
'End Those Muslims.'" Religion News Service, December 5, 2015.
https://religionnews.com/2015/12/05/jerry-falwell-jr-is-wrong-to
-encourage-concealed-weapons-to-end-those-muslims/.

Claiborne, Shane, and Michael Martin. *Beating Guns: Hope for People Who
Are Weary of Violence*. Grand Rapids: Brazos, 2019.

Coates, Ta-Nehisi. "Stand Your Ground and Vigilante Justice." *Atlantic*, March 22, 2012. http://www.theatlantic.com/national/ar
chive/2012/03/stand-your-ground-and-vigilante-justice/254900/.

"Concealed Carry Killers." Violence Policy Center: Concealed Carry
Killers. Accessed July 23, 2019. http://concealedcarrykillers.org/.

Cook, Philip J., and Kristin A. Goss. *The Gun Debate: What Everyone Needs
to Know*. Oxford: Oxford University Press, 2014.

Cook, Philip J., and Jens Ludwig. "The Limited Impact of the Brady Act."
In *Reducing Gun Violence in America: Informing Policy with Evidence
and Analysis*, edited by Daniel W. Webster and Jon S. Vernick,
21–32. Baltimore: Johns Hopkins University Press, 2013.

Copan, Paul, and Matt Flannagan. *Did God Really Command Genocide?
Coming to Terms with the Justice of God*. Grand Rapids: Baker Books,
2014.

Curry, Erin. "Hostage Reads 'Purpose-Driven Life' to Alleged Atlanta Killer." *Baptist Press*, March 14, 2005. http://www.bpnews
.net/20340/hostage-reads-purposedriven-life-to-alleged-atlan
ta-killer.

DeBrabander, Firmin. *Do Guns Make Us Free? Democracy and the Armed
Society*. New Haven: Yale University Press, 2015.

DeGrazia, David. "Handguns, Moral Rights, and Physical Security."
Journal of Moral Philosophy 13 (2014): 1–21.

DeGrazia, David, and Lester H. Hunt. *Debating Gun Control: How Much
Regulation Do We Need?* New York: Oxford University Press, 2016.

DeYoung, Rebecca Konyndyk. "Courage." In *Being Good: Christian Virtues for Everyday Life*, edited by Michael W. Austin and R. Douglas Geivett, 145–66. Grand Rapids: Eerdmans, 2012.

Diamond, Jeremy, and Tom LoBianco. "Donald Trump: Obama Considering Executive Order to Take Guns Away." *CNN*, October 20, 2015. https://www.cnn.com/2015/10/19/politics/donald-trump-guns-obama-south-carolina/index.html.

Diep, Francie. "Church Shootings Are Becoming Much More Common." *Pacific Standard*, November 6, 2017. https://psmag.com/news/church-shootings-are-becoming-much-more-common.

Disney, Abigail. *The Armor of Light*. Documentary. Samuel Goldwyn Films, 2015.

District of Columbia v. Heller. 554 U.S. 570 (2008).

Educational Fund to Stop Gun Violence, The. "New CDC Data Show That Nearly 40,000 People Died by Guns in 2017." News release, December 7, 2018. https://efsgv.org/press-archive/2018/cdc-shows-increase-in-gun-deaths-in-2017/.

Edwards, James R. *The Gospel according to Luke*. Grand Rapids: Eerdmans, 2015.

Ehrenfreund, Max. "Why So Many Americans Think the Government Wants Their Guns." *Washington Post*, January 8, 2016. https://www.washingtonpost.com/news/wonk/wp/2016/01/08/why-so-many-americans-think-the-government-wants-their-guns/.

"11 Times a Good Guy with a Gun Stopped a Bad Guy, Saving Lives." Photo gallery. *Washington Times*. Accessed July 23, 2019. https://www.washingtontimes.com/multimedia/collection/good-guy-gun-stopped-bad-guy-gun/.

Erler, Edward J. "The Second Amendment as an Expression of First Principles." *Imprimis* 42, no. 3 (March 2013). https://imprimis.hillsdale.edu/the-second-amendment-as-an-expression-of-first-principles/.

Fabbre, Alicia, and Vikki Ortiz Healy. "Pastor's Son Accidentally Shoots, Kills Teen Cousin in Will County; Police Say No Charges Expected." *Chicago Tribune*, December 27, 2018. https://www.chicagotribune.com/suburbs/ct-met-juvenile-shot-willmington-church-20171227-story.html.

Fagan, Andrew. "Human Rights." Internet Encyclopedia of Philosophy. Accessed July 23, 2019. http://www.iep.utm.edu/hum-rts/#SH3a.

Farrell, Kevin J. "A Response to Open Carry." Bishop Kevin Farrell, January 5, 2016. https://bishopkevinfarrell.org/2016/01/open-carry/.

"Firearm Justifiable Homicides and Non-Fatal Self-Defense Gun Use: An Analysis of Federal Bureau of Investigation and National Crime Victimization Survey Data." Violence Policy Center, May 2017.

Fitzmyer, Joseph A. *The Gospel according to Luke X–XXIV: Introduction, Translation, and Notes*. Garden City, NY: Doubleday, 1985.

Fleischer, Matthew Curtis. *The Old Testament Case for Nonviolence*. Oklahoma City: Epic Octavius the Triumphant, 2017.

"Fully Protected Bible Study." Dietrich Bonhoeffer Institute. Accessed July 23, 2019. https://tdbi.org/resources/fully-protected-bible-study/.

Galli, Mark. "God Hates Gun Violence." *Christianity Today*, May 18, 2018. https://www.christianitytoday.com/ct/2018/june/god-hates-gun-violence.html.

Green, Joel B. *The Gospel of Luke*. New International Commentary on the New Testament. Grand Rapids: Eerdmans, 1997.

Green, Joel B., Scot McKnight, and I. Howard Marshall, eds. *Dictionary of Jesus and the Gospels*. Downers Grove, IL: IVP Academic, 1992.

"Greene County, Virginia GOP Group's Newsletter Calls for 'Armed Revolution' If Obama Is Reelected." *Huffington Post*, May 8, 2012, updated December 6, 2017. https://www.huffingtonpost.com/2012/05/08/greene-county-virginia-gop-obama-revolution_n_1501510.html.

Grudem, Wayne. *Christian Ethics: An Introduction to Biblical Moral Reasoning*. Wheaton, IL: Crossway, 2018.

———. *Politics according to the Bible: A Comprehensive Resource for Understanding Modern Political Issues in Light of Scripture*. Grand Rapids: Zondervan, 2010.

Guardini, Romano. *The Lord*. Washington, DC: Gateway Editions, 1996.

"Gun Control and the Bible." Conservative Christians of Alabama. Accessed July 23, 2019. http://www.ccofal.org/alabama/what-does-the-bible-verses-say-about-gun-control.html.

Haag, Matthew. "Man Killed by Police at Alabama Mall Was a 'Good Guy with a Gun,' Family's Lawyer Says." *New York Times*, November 26, 2018. https://www.nytimes.com/2018/11/26/us/black-man-killed-alabama-mall-shooting.html.

Haag, Pamela. *The Gunning of America*. New York: Basic Books, 2016.

Hall, Christopher A. *Living Wisely with the Church Fathers*. Downers Grove, IL: IVP Academic, 2017.

Handy, Bruce. "'The Armor of Light' Is a Documentary That Explores the Intersection of Christianity and Guns." *Vanity Fair*, November 16, 2015. https://www.vanityfair.com/hollywood/2015/11/the-armor-of-light-documentary-christianity-guns.

Harper, Cynthia, and Sara McLanahan. "Father Absence and Youth Incarceration." *Journal of Research on Adolescence* 14 (2004): 369–97.

Harsanyi, David. "Why Bringing a Gun to Church Is a Pretty Good Idea." *Federalist*, November 7, 2017. http://thefederalist.com/2017/11/07/bringing-gun-church-pretty-good-idea/.

Hays, Richard B. *The Moral Vision of the New Testament: Community, Cross, New Creation; A Contemporary Introduction to New Testament Ethics*. San Francisco: HarperOne, 1996.

Hemenway, David. "Does Owning a Gun Make You Safer?" *Los Angeles Times*, August 4, 2015. http://www.latimes.com/opinion/op-ed/la-oe-0804-hemenway-defensive-gun-home-20150730-story.html.

———. *Private Guns, Public Health*. Rev. ed. Ann Arbor: University of Michigan Press, 2017.

"Heroes Risk Their Lives to Stop Mass Shootings. Lawmakers Don't Have the Guts to Pass Gun Reform." Editorial, *Washington Post*, May 8, 2019. https://www.washingtonpost.com/opinions/heroes-risk-their-lives-to-stop-mass-shootings-lawmakers-dont-have-the-guts-to-pass-gun-reform/2019/05/08/990d9abe-71cb-11e9-8be0-ca575670e91c_story.html.

Howard, Bernard. "A Christian Case for Gun Control." *Mere Orthodoxy*, June 22, 2016. https://mereorthodoxy.com/christian-case-gun-control/.

Howard, Jacqueline. "Gun Deaths in US Reach Highest Level in Nearly 40 Years, CDC Data Reveal." *CNN*, December 14, 2018. https://www.cnn.com/2018/12/13/health/gun-deaths-highest-40-years-cdc/index.html.

Hsiao, Timothy. "Against Gun Bans and Restrictive Licensing." *Essays in Philosophy* 16, no. 2 (2015): 180–203. https://doi.org/10.7710/1526-0569.1531.

Hubbard, Moyer. "'Let the One Who Has No Sword, Buy One': The

Biblical Argument for Gun Control, Part Two." *Good Book Blog*, February 25, 2014. https://www.biola.edu/blogs/good-book -blog/2014/let-the-one-who-has-no-sword-buy-one-the-biblical -argument-for-gun-control-part-two.

Huckabee, Mike. *God, Guns, Grits, and Gravy*. New York: St. Martin's Griffin, 2016.

Huemer, Michael. "Is There a Right to Own a Gun?" *Social Theory and Practice* 29, no. 2 (2003): 297–324.

Hutchinson, Mira. "Mike Huckabee: If Only Someone in That Church Had Been Carrying a Gun Too." *Hinterland Gazette*, June 19, 2015. https://hinterlandgazette.com/2015/06/mike-huckabee-charles ton-church-shooting-concealed-weapon.html.

"In Guns We Trust." Editorial. *Christianity Today*, October 4, 1999. https:// www.christianitytoday.com/ct/1999/october4/in-guns-we-trust -fear-idolatry.html.

Jenkins, Jack. "Lawmakers Calling for More Guns in Church Have a The- ology Problem." *Think Progress*, November 6, 2017. https://think progress.org/guns-church-theology-problem-0cde29cf72f8/.

Johnson, David Kyle. "Fallacy: All or Nothing." In *Bad Arguments: 100 of the Most Important Fallacies in Western Philosophy*, edited by Robert Arp, Steven Barbone, and Michael Bruce. Oxford: Wiley Black- well, 2018. Available at https://www.academia.edu/21565174/Fal lacy_All_or_Nothing.

Johnson, Kimberly. "Carolina Congregations Wrestle with Taking Guns to Church." *Aljazeera America*, August 31, 2015. http://america .aljazeera.com/articles/2015/8/31/carolina-guns-in-churches.html.

Keener, Craig S. *The Gospel of Matthew: A Socio-Rhetorical Commentary*. Grand Rapids: Eerdmans, 2009.

Keneally, Meghan. "Breaking Down the NRA-Backed Theory That a Good Guy with a Gun Stops a Bad Guy with a Gun." *ABC News*, October 29, 2018. http://abcnews.go.com/US/breaking-nra -backed-theory-good-guy-gun-stops/story?id=53360480.

"Key Gun Violence Statistics." Brady Campaign to Prevent Gun Vio- lence. Accessed July 23, 2019. http://www.bradycampaign.org /key-gun-violence-statistics.

King, Martin Luther. "Martin Luther King Jr.—Acceptance Speech." Nobel Prize, December 10, 1964. https://www.nobelprize.org

/prizes/peace/1964/king/26142-martin-luther-king-jr-acceptance
-speech-1964/.

Kleck, Gary, and Marc Gertz. "Armed Resistance to Crime: The Prevalence and Nature of Self-Defense with a Gun." *Journal of Criminal
Law and Criminology* 86, no. 1 (1995): 150–87.

Kopel, David B. *The Morality of Self-Defense and Military Action: The Judeo-Christian Tradition.* Santa Barbara, CA, and Denver: Praeger,
2017.

Lacayo, Richard. "Under Fire." *Time,* June 24, 2001. http://content.time
.com/time/magazine/article/0,9171,153695,00.html.

Lactantius. *Divine Institutes.* Book 4, chap. 20. New Advent. Accessed July
23, 2019. http://www.newadvent.org/fathers/07016.htm.

LaFollette, Hugh. *In Defense of Gun Control.* New York: Oxford University
Press, 2018.

Lampe, G. W. H. "The Two Swords (Luke 22:35–38)." In *Jesus and the
Politics of His Day*, edited by Ernst Bammel and C. F. D. Moule,
335–51. Cambridge: Cambridge University Press, 1984. https://doi
.org/10.1017/CBO9780511554834.

Leibovich, Mark. "Do Politicians' 'Thoughts and Prayers' Mean Anything?" *New York Times*, January 19, 2018. https://www.nytimes
.com/2015/10/18/magazine/do-politicians-thoughts-and-prayers
-mean-anything.html.

Le Miere, Jason. "Wayne LaPierre Slams 'Elites' in CPAC Speech Even
as He Earns $5 Million Annually from NRA." *Newsweek*, Febru-
ary 22, 2018. http://www.newsweek.com/wayne-lapierre-nra-cpac
-guns-816294.

Lewis, C. S. *Mere Christianity.* Revised and enlarged ed. San Francisco:
HarperOne, 2015.

Light, Caroline. *Stand Your Ground: A History of America's Love Affair with
Lethal Self-Defense.* Boston: Beacon, 2017.

Lindgren, James T., and Justin Lee Heather. "Counting Guns in Early
America." *William & Mary Law Review* 43, no. 5 (2002): 1777–1842.

Lott, John R. *More Guns, Less Crime: Understanding Crime and Gun Control
Laws.* 3rd ed. Chicago: University of Chicago Press, 2010.

Malina, Bruce J. *The New Testament World: Insights from Cultural Anthropol-
ogy.* Rev. ed. Louisville: Westminster John Knox, 1993.

Marsh, Charles. "The NRA's Assault on Christian Faith and Practice."

Religion & Politics, January 3, 2018. http://religionandpolitics
.org/2018/01/03/the-nras-assault-on-christian-faith-and-practice/.

Marshall, I. Howard. *The Gospel of Luke*. American ed. Grand Rapids: Eerdmans, 1978.

McDonald v. City of Chicago, Ill. 561 U.S. 742 (2010).

McKirdy, Euan, and Emanuella Grinberg. "Japan Knife Attack: At Least 19 Dead." *CNN*, updated July 26, 2016. https://www.cnn
.com/2016/07/25/world/japan-knife-attack-deaths/index.html.

McQuilkin, Robertson, and Paul Copan. *An Introduction to Biblical Ethics: Walking in the Way of Wisdom*. 3rd ed. Downers Grove, IL: IVP Academic, 2014.

Merritt, Jonathan. "Jerry Falwell Jr.'s Troubling Remarks on Guns." *Atlantic*, December 6, 2015. https://www.theatlantic.com/pol
itics/archive/2015/12/jerry-falwell-jrs-troubling-remarks-on
-guns/419019/.

Miller, Matthew, Deborah Azrael, and David Hemenway. "Firearms and Violent Death in the United States." In *Reducing Gun Violence in America: Informing Policy with Evidence and Analysis*, edited by Daniel W. Webster and Jon S. Vernick, 3–20. Baltimore: Johns Hopkins University Press, 2013.

Miller, Sharon Hodde. "Why All Christians Can Back Better Gun Control." *Christianity Today*, January 9, 2013. https://www.christian
itytoday.com/women/2013/january/why-all-christians-can-back
-better-gun-control.html.

Minear, Paul. "A Note on Luke XXII 36." *Novum Testamentum* 7 (1964): 128–34.

Moore, Russell. "Is Gun Control a Christian Issue?" Russell Moore, January 5, 2016. https://www.russellmoore.com/2016/01/05/is
-gun-control-a-christian-issue/.

Napolitano, Andrew P. "Guns and Freedom." *Fox News*, January 10, 2013, last updated May 11, 2015. https://www.foxnews.com/opinion
/guns-and-freedom.

National Center for Statistics and Analysis. "2017 Fatal Motor Vehicle Crashes: Overview." Washington, DC, 2018. https://crashstats
.nhtsa.dot.gov/Api/Public/ViewPublication/812603.

Neufeld, Thomas R. Yoder. *Killing Enmity: Violence and the New Testament*. Grand Rapids: Baker Academic, 2011.

Neville, David J. *The Vehement Jesus: Grappling with Troubling Gospel Texts.* Eugene, OR: Cascade, 2017.

Novak, Jake. "Stop Blaming the NRA for Failed Gun Control Efforts." *CNBC*, February 16, 2018. https://www.cnbc.com/2018/02/16/nra -money-isnt-why-gun-control-efforts-are-failing-commentary .html.

Orend, Brian. *The Morality of War.* 2nd ed. Peterborough, ON, and Buffalo: Broadview, 2013.

Parker, Kim, Juliana Menasce Horowitz, Ruth Igielnik, J. Baxter Oliphant, and Anna Brown. "America's Complex Relationship with Guns." Pew Research Center, June 22, 2017. https://www .pewsocialtrends.org/2017/06/22/americas-complex-relation ship-with-guns/.

"Past Summary Ledgers." Gun Violence Archive. Accessed July 23, 2019. https://www.gunviolencearchive.org/past-tolls.

Piper, John. "Should Christians Be Encouraged to Arm Themselves?" *Desiring God*, December 22, 2015. https://www.desiringgod.org /articles/should-christians-be-encouraged-to-arm-themselves.

"Police: Masked Gunman Killed by Alabama McDonald's Customer." Associated Press, October 29, 2018. https://apnews.com/86e53d 649683429188b3e3f79dd398b8.

Polsby, Daniel, and Don Kates. "Of Holocausts and Gun Control." *Washington University Law Quarterly* 75 (1997): 1237–75.

Powers, Kirsten, and Jonathan Merritt. "Christians, Guns and the Mass Shooting Epidemic." *The Faith Angle* (podcast), *Relevant*, April 3, 2018. https://relevantmagazine.com/podcast/chris tians-guns-mass-shooting-epidemic/.

Raab, Joseph Quinn. "Comrades for Peace: Thomas Merton, the Dalai Lama and the Preferential Option for Nonviolence." *Merton Annual* 19 (2006): 255–66.

Rae, Scott. *Moral Choices: An Introduction to Ethics.* 4th ed. Grand Rapids: Zondervan, 2018.

Reilly, Katie. "'Thoughts and Prayers Are Not Enough.' Democrats Demand Action after Texas Shooting." *Time*, November 6, 2017. http://time.com/5011550/texas-church-shooting-thoughts -prayers-gun-control/.

Relman, Eliza. "Megachurch Pastor on 'Fox & Friends' Says His Parishioners Could Stop a Shooting Because They Carry Guns into Church." *Business Insider*, November 6, 2017. https://www .businessinsider.com/megachurch-pastor-fox-friends-guns-con cealed-carry-2017-11.

Rensberger, David. "Jesus's Action in the Temple." In *Struggles for Shalom: Peace and Violence across the Testaments*, edited by Laura L. Brenneman and Brad D. Schantz, 179–90. Eugene, OR: Pickwick, 2014.

Reyes-Chow, Bruce. "Why This Christian Will Never Own a Gun." *Red Letter Christians*, August 30, 2012. https://www.redletterchristians .org/why-this-christian-will-never-own-a-gun/.

Rhee, Joseph, Tahman Bradley, and Brian Ross. "U.S. Military Weapons Inscribed with Secret 'Jesus' Bible Codes." *ABC News*, January 18, 2010. https://abcnews.go.com/Blotter/us-military-weapons -inscribed-secret-jesus-bible-codes/story?id=9575794.

Sandlin, P. Andrew. Post for Bill Blankschaen. "Pistol Packin' Jesus: A Response to Shane Claiborne." *Patheos*, December 15, 2015. https://www.patheos.com/blogs/faithwalkers/2015/12/pistol -packin-jesus-a-response-to-shane-claiborne/.

Schenck, Rob. *Costly Grace: An Evangelical Minister's Rediscovery of Faith, Hope, and Love*. New York: Harper, 2018.

Shapiro, Emily. "During Discussion about Guns in Church, Man Accidentally Shoots Himself, Wife: Police." *ABC News*, November 17, 2017. https://abcnews.go.com/US/man-acciden tally-shoots-wife-church-discussing-weapons-churches/sto ry?id=51221000.

Shribman, David. "How Guns Became Such a Deeply Ingrained Part of the American Identity." *Globe and Mail*, February 25, 2018, updated February 27, 2018. https://www.theglobeandmail.com /news/world/us-politics/how-guns-became-part-of-the-ameri can-identity/article38108238/.

Skibba, Ramin. "Researchers Tackle Gun Violence Despite Lack of Federal Funding." *NPR*, May 12, 2018. https://www.npr.org/sections /health-shots/2018/05/12/609701029/researchers-tackle-gun-vio lence-despite-lack-of-federal-funding.

Smith, David Livingstone. *Less Than Human: Why We Demean, Enslave, and Exterminate Others*. New York: St. Martin's, 2011.

Sparks, Elicka Peterson. *The Devil You Know: The Surprising Link between Conservative Christianity and Crime*. Amherst, NY: Prometheus, 2016.

Stassen, Glen, and David Gushee. *Kingdom Ethics: Following Jesus in Contemporary Context*. Downers Grove, IL: IVP Academic, 2003.

Stevens, John Paul. "John Paul Stevens: Repeal the Second Amendment." *New York Times*, March 28, 2018. https://www.nytimes.com/2018/03/27/opinion/john-paul-stevens-repeal-second-amendment.html.

"Study Finds States with Most Gun Laws Have Fewest Gun Deaths But . . ." *WBUR* (Boston), March 13, 2013. https://www.wbur.org/hereandnow/2013/03/13/gun-laws-study.

Suttle, Tim. "Why Do American Christians Trust the 2nd Amendment More Than the Sermon on the Mount?" *Patheos*, July 9, 2016. https://www.patheos.com/blogs/paperbacktheology/2016/07/why-do-american-christians-trust-the-2nd-amendment-more-than-the-sermon-on-the-mount.html.

Tanner, Lindsey. "Guns Send over 8,000 US Kids to ER Each Year, Analysis Says." Associated Press, October 28, 2018. https://www.apnews.com/b806812a8f0945128b4c5e47a9f3c739.

Trivigno, Franco. "A Virtue Ethical Case for Pacifism." In *Virtues in Action: New Essays in Applied Virtue Ethics*, edited by Michael W. Austin, 86–101. New York: Palgrave Macmillan, 2013.

"2018 Florida Statutes, The." Sunshine Online. Accessed July 23, 2019. http://www.leg.state.fl.us/Statutes/index.cfm?App_mode=Display_Statute&URL=0700-0799/0776/0776.html.

Waldman, Michael. *The Second Amendment: A Biography*. New York: Simon & Schuster, 2015.

Webster, Daniel W., and Jon S. Vernick, eds. *Reducing Gun Violence in America: Informing Policy with Evidence and Analysis*. Baltimore: Johns Hopkins University Press, 2013.

———. "Spurring Responsible Firearms Sales Practice through Litigation." In *Reducing Gun Violence in America: Informing Policy with Evidence and Analysis*, edited by Daniel W. Webster and Jon S. Vernick, 21–32. Baltimore: Johns Hopkins University Press, 2013.

Weeks, Linton. "The First Gun in America." *NPR*, April 6, 2013. https://www.npr.org/2013/04/06/176132730/the-first-gun-in-america.

Whitehead, Andrew, Landon Schnabel, and Samuel Perry. "Why Some Christians Don't Believe in Gun Control: They Think God Handed Down the Second Amendment." *Washington Post*, July 25, 2018. https://www.washingtonpost.com/news/acts-of-faith/wp/2018/07/25/why-some-christians-dont-believe-in-gun-control-they-think-god-handed-down-the-second-amendment/.

Willard, Dallas. *The Divine Conspiracy: Rediscovering Our Hidden Life in God*. San Francisco: Harper, 1998.

———. *Renovation of the Heart: Putting On the Character of Christ*. Colorado Springs: NavPress, 2002.

Williams, Chris. "The Strange Love Affair between Christians and Guns." *Patheos*, June 14, 2016. https://www.patheos.com/blogs/chrisicisms/2016/06/14/christians-and-guns/.

Wintemute, Garen J. "Broadening Denial Criteria for the Purchase and Possession of Firearms." In *Reducing Gun Violence in America: Informing Policy with Evidence and Analysis*, edited by Daniel W. Webster and Jon S. Vernick, 77–93. Baltimore: Johns Hopkins University Press, 2013.

Yamane, David. "Awash in a Sea of Faith and Firearms: Rediscovering the Connection between Religion and Gun Ownership in America." *Journal for the Scientific Study of Religion* 55, no. 3 (September 2016): 622–36. https://doi.org/10.1111/jssr.12282.

———. "A Counterargument to 'Virtue and Guns.'" *Psychology Today*, May 24, 2019. https://www.psychologytoday.com/blog/ethics-everyone/201905/counterargument-virtue-and-guns.

———. "The Sociology of U.S. Gun Culture." *Sociology Compass* 11, no. 7 (July 1, 2017): e12497. https://doi.org/10.1111/soc4.12497.

Yan, Holly. "Hero Customer Rushes Waffle House Killer and Rips Away His Assault-Style Rifle." *CNN*, April 23, 2018. https://cnnphilippines.com/world/2018/04/23/Waffle-House-hero.html.

INDEX OF NAMES AND SUBJECTS

INDEX OF SCRIPTURE REFERENCES